THERE
ARE NO
LIMITS

Breaking the Barriers in
Personal High Performance

THERE ARE NO LIMITS

Breaking the Barriers in Personal High Performance

By
Danny Cox

There Are No Limits
Copyright © 2006 by Danny Cox

DANNY COX
ACCELERATIONIST®
17381 Bonner Drive, Suite 101
Tustin, CA 92780
Phone: 1-800-366-3101
Fax: 1-714-838-1869
E-mail: Danny@DannyCox.com
Website: www.DannyCox.com

Published by
Executive Books
206 West Allen Street
Mechanicsburg, PA 17055
717-766-9499 800-233-2665
Fax: 717-766-6565
www.ExecutiveBooks.com

ISBN: 0-937539-96-1

Library of Congress Cataloging-in-Publication Data

Cox, Danny, 1934-
    There are no limits: breaking the barriers in personal high performance
by Danny Cox.
    p.   cm.
    1. Self-actualization (Psychology)   I. Title
BF637.S4C7   1998
158.1--dc21   98-16985

Cover Design by Kat Casey
Interior Layout by Gregory A. Dixon

Printed in the United States of America

DEDICATION

To my daughters, Lisa, Kendra, and Darcie, as well as my grandchildren, Lauren, Ryan, Rex, Kenny, Kristy Beth, Dominic, Kameron and Isabella. May this book help you in your quest for "no limits" lives.

ACKNOWLEDGMENTS

At this writing, I'm in Istanbul, Turkey, to speak to 700 Turkish executives, their employees, and salespeople in a program sponsored by the *Executive Excellence Newsletter*, published here. From my window, I see the Bosporus Strait that divides this ancient city into two parts, with one part in Europe and the other in Asia. Twelve different civilizations have left their imprint on this remarkable country.

It's a fitting place, on this rainy afternoon, to reflect on the people who have left their imprint on me and my life. I thank them for that.

First, thank you to the "no limits" people (my mentors) who shared their "barrier-breaking" secrets with me. I'm certain that, at some of those sessions, they were seeing more potential in me than I was seeing in myself at the time. Fortunately for me, they knew anyone could lead a "no limits" life if he or she wanted to badly enough. I deeply appreciate their techniques, ideas, and encouragement they so freely shared. The two standouts in this category are Jim and Ellie Newton.

Next, my heartfelt thanks to my wife, Theo, who has not only shared her life with me for more than three decades, but was a sounding board and an idea generator for this project. Without her help, this book would not be a reality.

To Brandon Toropov, who took all of this information, organized it, and "nailed it down" on paper, I say, "Thank you, thank you, thank you!" Your professionalism and enthusiasm made you a delight to work with.

CONTENTS

Part 4—Your Desire for Continued Personal Growth

A Fantasy
Gathering of
No-limits Thinkers

[The following is a fictional account.]

The snow was falling that night in early 1901 as four good friends met at their favorite inn. The talk of all the newspapers and magazines was of the new century—the 20th century—but these four gentlemen had something very different on their minds. As they sat around the table in front of a large stone fireplace, they stared at a question one of the four had written on a card and placed at the center of the table:

"What will the world of the 21st century hold for our descendants?"

A bushy-haired man—the oldest of the group—was the first to attempt to answer the question. "I believe that when the year 2,000 dawns," he said, "men and women will have harnessed the power of electricity to accomplish things that the most daring of today's writers would scarcely admit to imagining. For instance, the men and women of the 21st century will calculate huge sums with absolute accuracy using tiny electric machines. They will fit the glorious sounds of the symphony into a device they can hold in the palm of a hand, and they will use miniature earpieces that will allow 20 people to listen to 20 different performances in a single room, each with perfect clarity. Our descendants will witness momentous events from across the globe the instant they occur, thanks to vivid, constantly changing electric portraits that transmit moving images from thousands of miles away."

The proprietor of the establishment, a glum fellow with a cynical look on his face, heard these words as he stood beside the fireplace, ready to throw another log on the fire, and shook his head sadly. "That Edison is a fool," he thought to himself, glancing at the man who had, a few decades earlier, opened the world's first central electric-light power plant. "He gets a good idea every now and then, but once he starts dreaming, he starts talking like a genuine madman. If he keeps this up, he's going to upset the rest of my guests."

Edison looked at the man to his left. The group followed his lead and turned its attention to an intense, thin-faced fellow in his mid-30s. "Well, Tom, I've been thinking about starting up an automobile business. As you know, a few years back, I built my first car in my spare time. What a marvelous machine! I believe this technology will change the face of our world so dramatically that, within two or three decades, most cities will be unrecognizable—and by the time the next century dawns, I believe every family in our country will either own or have easy access to a private automobile. I believe that great highways will open up the nation to people of even modest means. And I believe that the automobile will enable people to live far from the cities if they wish, without losing access to any of the conveniences within the cities."

"There goes that Ford again, shooting his mouth off," the proprietor thought to himself. "Always babbling on about how his hobby is going to change the nation. It's a good thing that man's not in charge of anything important." He polished a glass and placed it on the counter. The proprietor stared around the room, wondering whether his customers were eavesdropping on this ridiculous conversation, as he was. As he'd feared, a few had stopped eating and were staring at Edison and his friends, including a family at the table closest to them. The mother and the father were listening intently, and their wide-eyed 10-year-old son, who had already read quite a bit about the great Edison, was hanging on every word.

Edison's group turned its attention to a man slightly younger than the automobile enthusiast, a handsome fellow with a clear gaze and a winning smile. This man had been nodding briskly as Henry Ford had spoken, and after the group murmured its approval for Ford's prediction, the optimistic-looking man sitting next to him spoke up. "I believe Henry's right," the man with the smile said. "I believe the automobile will change the way this country—and the entire world— lives. I also believe whole new industries will thrive as never before as a result of the automobile's success, and I aim for my own industry to be one of them. To be quite honest, I feel Henry's going to show us all how to use machines to develop companies that are far more efficient, far more profitable, and far more successful than they are today. And I'll go further. I believe that, by the end of this century, our children and grandchildren will have so thoroughly mastered the arts of technology, invention, and engineering that they will even consider journeys beyond our world, trips to the moon, and mechanized explorations of other planets to be rather ordinary and predictable things."

The proprietor shook his head in disbelief at the bizarre and outlandish conversation. Even though the last speaker, Harvey Firestone, was a man of experience and accomplishment, a leader in the American rubber industry, the thought of people believing something as outlandish as space travel to be routine was downright laughable. "How strange that a man as distinguished as that Firestone," the proprietor thought to himself, "should be enough of a madman to believe such undertakings to be possible. If humanity is meant to journey beyond the earth, it will only be from the pages of books of fiction!"

Finally, the fourth friend, a young French doctor, addressed the question. He had a calm face and a strangely confident air. When he spoke, he did so with a sense of deep certainty that had somehow eluded the others—as though he himself were somehow privy to the inner workings of the future. "There is both terrible trauma and extraordinary achievement awaiting our children, grandchildren, and great-grandchildren. There will be wars of unspeakable cruelty—but the great powers will eventually learn to make peace as a result of having endured them, and human medicine will improve immeasurably as a result of those wars. There will be diseases and injuries on a level we cannot now imagine—but we will eventually learn to cure many more of the sick and heal many more of the injured than we can today. We will learn to rebuild the lives of men, women, and children who today would die from smallpox, polio, heart disease, and scores of other ailments—and we will even learn to replace hearts, kidneys, and other organs in order to prolong life."

The proprietor stared at the young man who made these bold predictions and realized that, although the whole gathering at that strange table was nodding in agreement, the rest of the people in the dining room were dumbfounded. Some were laughing. Some were shaking their heads.

"So Edison's companions," he thought to himself, "have all finally taken leave of their senses, even that young Carrel fellow, who had seemed so sensible when he walked in." [Alexis Carrel was awarded the Nobel Prize in 1912 for his work in suturing blood vessels and in pioneering organ transplants. In 1938, he developed the perfusion pump—an early artificial heart—with Charles Lindbergh.]

Oblivious to the stares of his fellow diners at other tables, Edison nodded enthusiastically at Carrel's remarks. Then he said, "Friends, this has been a stimulating discussion. I believe we each have a sense of what we'll need to do to help bring about the seeming miracles we've been discussing. But we still haven't done enough. The world will still need someone to help shrink the globe—someone who will show the world that geographical distance is only a perceived obstacle. Such a person would have to do something truly remarkable—something that would ignite the interest and adoration of the whole world at virtually the same instant. Perhaps he'll construct a flying machine and travel independently across an ocean. Whatever he does, he'll demonstrate that even physical borders and immense distances are not impediments to inspired achievement." [Charles Lindbergh was born in 1903.]

"In addition, I believe we'll need someone else—someone who can carry our message through to the 21st century, someone very special who will serve as a personal link from that time to this." [James Newton, friend and confidant to all the great men discussed in this foreword, was born in 1905. His insights are discussed in detail later on in this book.]

"But these are problems for another time," Edison continued. "What I want to say to you today, my friends, is that each of you now has the chance to..."

"Each of you is a dolt!" interrupted the proprietor, who could no longer contain himself. "Each of you is an addle-brained dreamer without an ounce of practical common sense. I've never heard such nonsense in my life! Symphonies in tiny boxes! Automobiles for every family! Journeys to the stars! Replacement hearts! Flying machines that leap over oceans! I've got half a mind to throw the four of you out of the place right now."

Mr. Edison smiled, bowed his head, and said quietly: "I had no idea our conversation was so objectionable to you."

"Your conversations with your friends are sometimes amusing, sir. But today you have gone too far. I will not have my inn turned into a haven for cranks. There are limits, Mr. Edison, there are limits."

A hush fell over the room as every diner looked at the four "cranks" seated at Mr. Edison's table.

The 10-year-old boy at the adjacent table rose and walked to Mr. Edison's side. The great inventor turned and two bright sets of eyes locked.

The boy said, "Mr. Edison, are there *really* limits?"

Edison got up from his chair, then bent to his knees so that he could look the little boy squarely in the face. He placed both hands on the boy's shoulders, and after a long pause, said emphatically, "Son, there are only the limits we place upon ourselves. It's when you look beyond those barriers that you see—*there are no limits!*"

Part 1:
Breaking Barriers

Chapter 1

Your New Birthday

"Apply yourself. Get all the education you can, but then, by God, do something! Don't just stand there—make something happen."
—Lee Iacocca

This is it—the moment you've been waiting for—your moment of glory. Your opportunity to put into action everything you've learned thus far in your life—and what you're about to learn in this guide to a "no limits" life.

We make a pretty big deal about the birthdays we find on our birth certificates. Those birthdays are good reasons for a party—but they're not the best reasons to celebrate. When you think about it, what did you really do to deserve a birthday party? You were born— you showed up! That's about it. You should really be throwing a party for your mother on that day, if you ask me!

Actually, I think each of us needs to pick a second birthday—to mark the day when we committed ourselves, consciously and completely, to becoming the best person we're capable of being, to developing our vast undeveloped potential. By the end of this book, I believe you'll be ready to make that special commitment.

When someone writes your biography, that person may have to devote one whole chapter to the day you decided, with full conviction, to take personal responsibility for developing all of your remaining potential. In my seminars, I encourage the people I'm training to write a declaration of personal responsibility, a special personalized document that marks the decision to take control of one's life.

Here's my declaration. May I suggest that you write your own?

Declaration of Personal Responsibility
by Danny Cox

I currently possess everything I've truly wanted and deserved. This is based on what I have handed out to date. My possessions, my savings, and my lifestyle are an exact mirror of me, my efforts, and my contribution to society. What I give, I get. If I am unhappy with what I have received it is because, as yet, I have not paid the required price. I have lingered too long in the "quibbling stage."

I fully understand that time becomes a burden to me only when it is empty. The past is mine and at this very moment I am purchasing another twenty-four hours of it. The future quickly becomes the past at a control point called the present moment. I not only truly live at that point, but I have full responsibility for the highest and best of the irreplaceable now.

I accept full responsibility for both the successes and failures in my life. If I am not what I desire to be at this point, what I am is my compromise. I no longer choose to compromise with my undeveloped potential.

I am the sum total of the choices I have made, and I continue to choose daily. What I now put under close scrutiny is the value of each upcoming choice. Therein lies the quality of my future life style.

Will my future belong to the "old me" or the "new me?" The answer depends on my attitude toward personal growth at this very moment. What time is left is all that counts, and that remaining time is my responsibility. With a newfound maturity, I accept full responsibility for how good I can become at what is most important to me.

With personal growth comes a fear of the unknown and new problems. Those problems are nothing more than the increasing shadow of my personal growth. I now turn my very real fear, with God's help, into a very real adventure.

My life now expands to meet my newfound destiny. "Old me," meet the "new me!"

Immediate Action: Describe your life 10 years from now. That's 3,650 days. Will they be 3,650 "reruns"—or will they be 3,650 days of purpose, adventure, and growth? How much joy will you be experiencing compared to right now? What form will that joy take? (Note: Expect your answers to change by the time you finish this book.)

Point to Ponder Before You Go On: "When what you've done in the past looks large to you, you haven't done much today."— Elbert Hubbard, American author of (among many other inspirational books) *A Message to Garcia,* one of the biggest-selling volumes of all time.

Chapter 2

The Crossroads

"Now is always beginning."
—Thomas Hornsby Ferril, author

E very day we stand at the "crossroads of our lives," which, if the truth be known, is a "Y" in the road. One path leads toward sameness—the other path leads toward no-limits living—living that is new, exciting, and adventurous.

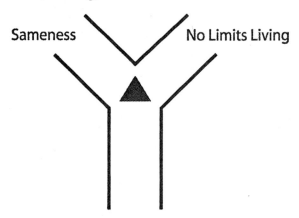

Sameness   No Limits Living

Every day there are decisions to be made about the directions we will take. And every day new opportunities for personal growth present themselves to us. Maybe we don't always see them, but they're there.

Those opportunities are there for you. Your personal crossroads represent unlimited possibilities to be explored, challenges to be met, and chances to experience life to its fullest. When we take full advantage of those opportunities, we overcome (imaginary) barriers—and prove to ourselves and anybody who's watching that there are no limits.

You may be asking yourself: How do I know when it's time to take that new direction? Which fork in that crossroads do I choose?

And how do I change direction again if things don't work out quite as well as I'd hoped? What if it ends up looking a whole lot like there are limits for me, after all? Answering those questions is what this book is all about.

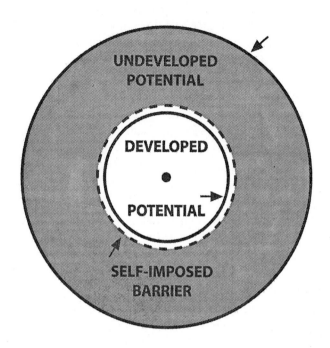

Take a look at the illustration above. The outer circle represents a person's full potential. When we're born, our developed potential is just a microscopic dot. Then we go to school and the circle gets to be a little bigger, and we start to have more experiences and the circle, again, gets a little bigger. We learn more things through new experiences, and the circle gets bigger still. And then, all too often, when we start a career, the expanding potential stops. We are left with a large area of unfulfilled potential. When we stop developing our potential, stop striving to fill up those circles of potential, we start to take the perceived barriers—that dotted line—for granted.

We often look at that division between the developed potential and the undeveloped potential as though it were a wall. But it's not; it's merely a boundary. To move past that dotted line, we must summon the steel inside ourselves.

Thomas Edison's widely quoted observation that "Genius is 1 percent inspiration and 99 percent perspiration" is often misunderstood. Because of this remark, many people think that Edison believed a life of toil and pain was necessary to produce breakthroughs. Nothing could be further from the truth. Edison *delighted* in his work, worked on things that delighted him, and was constantly inspired by the task of finding new ways to move past old barriers to take advantage of undeveloped potential. He enjoyed the process of impressing himself—of summoning the steel inside himself to move past what he had done before.

Everyone has a "steel thread" woven into the fabric of their being, whether it's discovered or undiscovered. What's yours? If you don't yet know (or don't remember) what your steel thread feels like, this book will help you pose the questions that will point you toward the answer.

Immediate Action: Keep reading!

Point to Ponder Before You Go On: "Successful [people] pay no attention to barriers, real or imaginary, erected by people or by customs. [They] persistently refuse to limit themselves, knowing the stagnating and destructive influence of restrictions....Those who limit themselves or others are not only engaging in a certain form of self-destruction, but are traitors to humanity and to the world....One need but choose whether he would take his place with the traitors or with the heroes."
—*Sherman J. Kline, author*

Chapter 3

"What Next?"

"Thought, not money, is the real business capital, and if you know, absolutely, that what you are doing is right, then you are bound to accomplish it in due season."
—Harvey Firestone

Maybe before you bought *There Are No Limits*, you saw one of my programs or read one of my other books or articles. If that's the case, you'd probably know that I worked in sales and sales management, and enjoyed some success in that field; nowadays, I'm a professional speaker. But before I did any of that, I spent 10 years flying supersonic fighters. I did air shows, as well as some test flying.

The airplane I flew was a big fighter, and one of my jobs was to test it out in the Arizona desert, as well as demonstrate its capabilities. This plane was 70 feet long, weighed 22-plus tons, and operated on 79,000 horsepower. That's three times the total horsepower of the Indianapolis 500—or 273 Porsche 911s.

It would go from sea level to 35,000 feet in one minute and 32 seconds. That's seven miles, straight up...in just a tad over a minute and a half! This plane was also capable of flying at 1,200 miles per hour. That's 20 miles per minute—one mile every three seconds—and seven football fields in *one* second.

Now, part of my job was to find holes in the radar net. So I would come across the Arizona desert at just 25 feet above the ground at 700 miles an hour (just under the speed of sound), pulling up over those saguaro cacti. Then I would climb way up 100 feet and fly supersonic. Well, one day, I received a call from the Thunderbirds. The gentleman on the other end of the line said, "We want to interview you for the team." It was a dream come true—or so I thought at the time.

I went through a six-hour interview with the Thunderbirds. At the end of the interview, the leader of the team walked over to me, put his hand out and said, "Congratulations! You made it!" I was elated. I had been invited to fly with the cream of the crop!

But it was not to be. You see, I was in the all-weather fighter group—the pilots who go up no matter how bad the weather is—and that's where the Air Force wanted me to stay. The Thunderbirds were in the day fighter group. I was needed most where I wanted to be least.

When I learned this, I said, "That's it. The Air Force has been asking for this, and they're going to get it. It's time for Plan B." Plan B, I told myself, would really shake up the Air Force and force them to back off the denial of my transfer—and, no doubt, toss in a letter of apology for good measure. Plan B was sending in my resignation.

They signed it.

Overnight, I was a civilian. And somehow I had to figure out what to do with the rest of my life. I had no money saved up. I had no retirement coming in. Nothing. A year and a half prior to this time, I had married—not the girl next door, as the story usually goes, but the beautiful young widow from across the street with three little girls. I got a real package deal when I got married!

Here I was, running out of air speed, altitude, and ideas all about same time. I don't know if you've ever been in one of those positions; a lot of people I meet before and after my speaking engagements sure have, though. I thought to myself, "Where am I going to go? What am I going to do?" I had gotten myself into a mess. Now how was I going to get myself out?

Fortunately, I ran into a good friend of mine, a guy by the name of Hal Needham. Maybe you know the name. He's the man who wrote and directed *Smokey and the Bandit* a few years back. When I first met him, though, he was a stunt man, falling off horses and wrecking cars for $500 a shot in the movies. When I told him about my situation, he said, "Get yourself to Southern California. If I can make it out there as a tree-trimmer from St. Louis with a 9th-grade education, surely you, the son of a coal miner from Marion, Illinois, ought to be able to make it."

So I followed Hal's advice and headed out to the West Coast. My idea at first was to fly with the airlines. I figured they would be excited to get a hold of the hottest thing in the skies. Wrong. It was fine as long as I was talking to them on the phone. "2,400 hours of high performance fighter time, test pilot, air show pilot, never had an accident?" they'd say. "Hey, that's the kind of guy we're looking for. We're mailing you an application today."

But I had already discovered that I had a problem with the airlines, and if you ever meet me in person, you'll know immediately what that problem is. I am, as the current phrase of the day has it, vertically challenged. Some people might say I'm short. Actually, the truth is, I'm just wound tight. Ever since my days on the college football and wrestling teams, I had the nickname "Mighty Mouse." I'm probably the only guy in the country who worked his way through college standing on wedding cakes! In the years since, I've tried to convince my tailor to make my pants about an inch too short so everyone can look at them and say, "Look how much he's grown since he bought that suit!"

So when the airline people offered to send me that application, I'd say, "Before you waste a stamp, what are the height requirements for flying with your airline?" They'd say, "Five foot eight." And I'd say, "What a coincidence! That happens to be my goal."

And that would be that—they wouldn't hire me. It was no dice, time and again—despite all my flying experience, despite my safety record, despite the fact that I could reach everything in the cockpit.

You see, the real problem was that they didn't want passengers leaning out in the aisle saying, "That little guy is going to fly this big airplane?" They were equating ability with size—something I don't think they can do anymore. It was pretty frustrating. I was tempted to form an antidiscrimination group, which I was going to call SPOT— Short People On Top. But that's another story. After knocking on any number of doors and making any number of depressing phone calls, I had to conclude that what I had done so well in the past—fly airplanes—didn't look like it was going to be part of my future.

What was next?

Immediate Action: Think about the last time you faced a change that seemed to be for the worst—but turned out to be for the best. Often, we face times that seem, for all the world, like the worst times of our lives—but they turn out to lead to some of the best. If you are now saying, "I am at that low point right now," then hang on and keep reading.

Point to Ponder Before You Go On: "Think or swim!"—John Stevens, American inventor. (And note, too, that Henry Ford once observed that "Thinking must be the hardest thing in the world to do—because so few people do it!")

Chapter 4

The Return of the Sonic Boom Salesman

"You start a journey both outward and inward. To make such a crossing, you escape the old nemesis and create a greater one. You give everything and receive everything."
—From *Threshold: The Blue Angels Experience*, by Frank Herbert

I was still stuck, and I thought, "My gosh. Where am I going to go and what am I going to do now?" I'd never let my height stand in my way before, and I didn't much feel like starting now. What else was open to me?

So I thought things over, and it occurred to me to try sales. I had already earned the title of "Sonic Boom Salesman" back when I was flying. After inadvertently knocking off more than my share of plaster and breaking more than my share of windows, I would then return and explain to some rather upset and hostile civilian audiences why these sonic booms were good for them. Those meetings with the locals could get pretty intense.

If you're a salesperson who's wondering how to deal with a difficult prospect, let me assure you that things could be worse. You may think that you have sold a product with a high-objection factor. Try selling sonic booms sometime!

I figured that if I could sell sonic booms, I could sell anything. So I joined a sales company and sold for a year.

At the end of a year, I looked at what I had earned and thought to myself, "Not bad. I made more in selling than I ever earned as a test pilot on hazardous duty pay, and I didn't have to worry about getting killed, either." Actually, that wasn't strictly true; I have to admit, there were a couple of customers that year who made me a bit nervous. But I'd made it through all right, and it was hard not to feel that I was on the right track once again.

At that point, my boss came to me and said, "You have a year of selling under your belt. Now we'd like you to manage one of our sales offices."

"Okay," I said, "Starting when?"

"This afternoon."

Well, my first thought was, "Obviously it doesn't take long to get to be a leader of salespeople." But there was more to come.

"Don't go out there to that office right now," I was told.

"Why not?" I asked.

"Well, Joe Schmoe (he was the current manager) is in that office right now, which is unusual because we usually aren't able to find him. Anyway, we've got to go run out there and fire him and get him cleared out so there won't be a big stink when you walk in. Give us a couple of hours."

That's a true story. I got some introduction to management, didn't I? Something should have told me I was walking into a bad situation; the manager in that office I was about to inherit had just been cut into narrow strips.

The story gets even more interesting. I went out there and for a year I sat in that manager's office, behind the manager's desk, and (in case there was any doubt) wore a name tag that said, "Danny Cox, Manager." Obviously, I was the manager. I had no idea what I was doing, but make no mistake about it, I was the manager. And even though I sometimes felt so mixed up that I didn't know whether to wind my head or scratch my watch, my office did all right.

A year later, the company came back to me and said, "Danny, you've got one year of managing under your belt. We would now like you to take over our top office—the number-one performer in our 36-office chain."

"How quickly you folks notice leadership talent," I said.

Bear in mind, now, that I had no idea at all about what I was doing. I didn't know what I didn't know. I was essentially improvising my way through everything, assuming that everyone would and should approach problems exactly as I had when I was a salesperson. I figured, though, that the people at the top of the company had to know that there was something in what I was doing that was working—otherwise, why would they make a risky move like promoting me? If I really didn't have any notion of how to manage people yet, promoting me would be, well, stupid. Wouldn't it?

Immediate Action: Think of a time when you should have realized you were "riding for a fall." Did you hear a still, small voice inside warning you about problems ahead?

Point to Ponder Before You Go On: Are you a pebble or a seed? That is, are you resting on your laurels, operating by rote, obeying the force of gravity—or are you consciously expanding your talents and moving upward to become something new, better, and far more exciting?

Chapter 5

A Prayer for Radiance

"Conscious power exists within the mind of everyone."
—Melles, French author

Here's a prayer of interest to all:

"I wish to be simple, honest, natural, frank, clean in mind and clean in body, unaffected—ready to say 'I do not know,' if so it be, to meet all [people] on an absolute equality—to face any obstacle and meet every difficulty unafraid and unabashed. I wish to live without hate, whim, jealousy, envy, or fear. I wish others to live their lives, too—up to their highest, fullest, and best. To that end I pray that I may never meddle, dictate, interfere, give advice that is not wanted, nor assist when my services are not needed. If I can help people, I will do it by giving them a chance to help themselves; and if I can uplift or inspire, let it be by example, inference, and suggestion, rather than by injunction and dictation. I desire to Radiate Life!"
—Elbert Hubbard

Immediate Action: Read this prayer again, and think about ways to apply it to various parts of your own life.

Point to Ponder Before You Go On: With the right values and a commitment to improve yourself before others, you can overcome even the most daunting obstacles and career setbacks. (See the next chapter for an example of this principle that's near and dear to my heart!)

Chapter 6

"Iceberg? What Iceberg?"

"Yours is a first-class mind, Prescott, but it does economy-class thinking."
—Cartoon caption in which senior businessperson berates a colleague during a business flight.

I could hardly wait to get back to the top office, because that's where I'd started out. That's where I'd been a brand new salesperson during the first year I was out of the Air Force. Just imagine how the top people in that office—who remembered me as the brand-new guy from the year before, the rookie from right out of the Air Force—would welcome me back as their boss. You guessed it. They hated me with a passion.

I kept saying to them, "Don't think of me as the boss. Think of me as a friend who's always right." (Ever work for one of those? I'm sure we all have, at one time or another.) Right there you can see where I made my big mistake. I wanted an office full of little Danny Coxes.

It seems to me that 99.9 percent of managers think, "My goal is to turn everybody who works for me into a copy of me," and for two very common reasons. The first reason is the tendency to think, "Isn't that what the company wants?" You know—people running around saying the same things and doing the same things. So the company wants everybody to think alike, dress alike, talk alike, and therefore I must have the company's blessing to turn everybody into little versions of me. Otherwise they'd put somebody different in the manager's chair—right?

But that's the smaller of the two common reasons. The bigger one is this: Managers say to themselves, "If I can get these people to do that job just exactly like I used to do that job, they'll never bring me a problem that I haven't already survived. Therefore, I will never be embarrassed with an unsolvable problem, and I will undoubtedly continue to be promoted up through company ranks." Now, isn't that a wonderful plan? It made sense to me! Well, I didn't know it, but I might as well have been the captain on the Titanic, bellowing, "Bring up the throttle!"

Don't bother me with any warnings about icebergs, thank you very much! I've got a job to do here! That was the way I thought when they made me a top gun, and I think you can imagine how well it worked. I took that office from first place—are you ahead of me?—to 36th out of 36 offices in just three months. If a competitor had planted a saboteur in that office, with orders to destroy any trace of productivity or profitability, I think it would have taken more than three months to get the job done as well as I did it. Then again, I was an insider with a hefty dose of managerial arrogance on my side. I had an advantage.

I had gone from a top gun to a son of a gun in no time, and the people who ran the company, quite naturally, wanted me out. The signs were certainly there. If you're a manager, and you start to pull into your parking lot in the morning only to find that your salespeople have arrived there before you and blocked all of the entrances with their cars—well, I guess that's the modern day version of circling the wagons like they did in the Old West. I reached the point where I was afraid to go out and stick my key in the ignition of the car until I had checked all of the wiring. Some nights, in fact, I would send my lowest sales producer out to test-start my car before I would get in it. It was the only incentive plan I had!

All right, maybe all that's an exaggeration, but it was clear I was in trouble. My boss came out to my office to deliver a terse little message through tight lips. He said, "I certainly made a mistake making you the manager and I feel it's only fair to let you know I'm now looking for your replacement."

"Well," I said, "That has got to be the shortest and the finest motivational seminar I have ever attended. I'll have to do something to turn this situation around."

"You don't have much time," he replied.

I said, "You have no idea how motivated I am."

So I went to work. But I went to work on me—not on the people who reported to me. As we said back home: "If you ain't got a choice—be brave!"

Immediate Action: Think about this: When has a manager tried to turn you into a miniature version of himself or herself? Did that tactic make it easier or more difficult for you to come to terms with the challenges you faced?

Point to Ponder Before You Go On: When we face a major challenge or temporary setback, reexamining our own behavior and strategies is almost always more effective than trying to change the habits of those who work with us.

Chapter 7

Signs of Trouble

"Pray for me."
—Shouted to the congregation by a misbehaving young child being carried to the exit by his father during church services.

You know you're in trouble at work when...
You regularly put your boss in a "horse-tossin' mood."
Your colleagues are about ready to comb your hair with a club.
Your boss calls you in for a 2 p.m. "tongue-lashing meeting" that takes up the remainder of the afternoon...and extends through the early portion of the evening.
Your customers write letters to the president of the company requesting permission to take you out of your office one piece at a time.
You come out the front door of the building wearing bits of glass.

Immediate Action: Think of the worst thing that ever happened to you at work. Did the sun come up, as scheduled, the next morning?

Point to Ponder Before You Go On: Temporary setbacks are part of every career—the trick is to keep them in perspective. Major setbacks are even bigger *and* better lessons for greater achievements in the future.

Chapter 8

Discovering
the Person

"The creation of a thousand forests is in an acorn."
—Ralph Waldo Emerson

S omerset Maugham, the great English author, once said, "Adversity puts iron in your flesh." Another one of my favorite authors, a man by the name of Orison Swett Marden, said, "Adversity sometimes strips a person, only to discover the person." Well, through adversity I discovered quite a lot about my person. I went back to square one and started learning not only about my own potential, but about the potential of the people who worked for me. And the biggest lesson I learned was that salespeople can get better—right after the sales manager does.

There are universal applications in that principle. Employees get better right after managers do. Kids get better right after parents do. Students get better right after teachers do. Audiences get better right after speakers do. Customers get better right after salespeople, sales managers, upper management, receptionists, secretaries, order clerks, and anybody else who happens to be in the company get better. That's a lesson we often learn the hard way, through adversity.

It turned out that I didn't lose my job. I started studying and listening to the people who worked for me, and I stopped trying to turn them into reproductions of myself. I started encouraging a more creative approach to the problems we faced. And 120 days later, we were back up to Number One.

That was a moment to be savored, not only because of the sense of achievement, but because it would then be possible to ease off a bit and relax after that incredible climb back to Number One. Or so I thought. There's a certain danger in taking that kind of attitude. If I had hung on to it, you know what would have happened, don't you?

Our sales would have plateaued back out and you'd be reading a book by some other author, not me!

Well, my salespeople and I started talking about this phenomenon. It can happen to anybody working in any job at any level: When you get to a certain way of doing your job, it's tempting to just quit getting better at it. That is what is called a self-imposed barrier. We'll be looking at that kind of barrier in greater detail a little later on in this book, but I want to take this opportunity to give you the introductory tour now.

Nobody builds a self-imposed barrier for you. You build it for yourself. A self-imposed barrier is not a wall around your life, it's just the margin of your life, where you stopped growing. These barriers can rise up at just about any level, whether it's low, medium, or even high productivity! (See illustration 2 in chapter 2.)

Immediate Action: Think of a time when you've told someone—perhaps a friend or family member—"Come on. You can do better than that." Did you ever hear that person reply, "No, I can't— I've never done this job better than that." The truth is, that's not a reason. That's not even a good excuse. It's only the flag atop the so-called barrier. It shows where the new potential starts.

Point to Ponder Before You Go On: Phillips Brooks, the minister who wrote "O Little Town of Bethlehem," had a powerful thought: "When you discover you've been leading only half a life, the other half is going to haunt you until you develop it." He was absolutely right!

No-limits thinking is the kind of thinking that's dedicated to finding a way to live a full life—so that the unexplored half of your identity, the half you can develop but don't, doesn't come back to haunt you.

Chapter 9

Check Your Six!

"Only a mediocre person is always at his best."
—Somerset Maugham

One time I was conducting a leadership program at a client's company headquarters in South Carolina. During the lunch break, as I was strolling around with one of their vice presidents, I couldn't help but notice the great inspirational quotes hanging on the walls. I commented that this was a great idea, whereupon this VP told me: "These are the philosophical tidbits we used in the turnaround we went through a few years ago. We were a very old company that had gotten in the doldrums and plateaued out. Then our CEO read a book by Philip Crosby called *Quality Is Free*—and after that we turned the company around. Now we're the acknowledged world leader in our field."

The first quote on the wall that really caught my eye said, "There is no saturation to education." What a great thought that is! Think about it. Do you realize that nobody has ever been completely educated? There is always room for another new idea! I think that quote ought to be on every manager's wall and across the top of every company newsletter: There is no saturation to education!

But the one that brought me to an absolute halt was a few yards further down the hallway. This is the one that will stick with me to the day I die: "Good is the enemy of best; best is the enemy of better." Wow! That's profound! When we get good at something, what do we tend to say? "Why do I have to be the best at this? I'm already good at it." Should we happen to become the best at something, then the tendency is to say, "Why do I need to get any better? I'm already Number One."

But it's when you're the best that you need to get better, more than any other time. Why is this? Because when contentment in the way you're doing your job sets in, progress and productivity plateau.

When I was in the cockpit of my fighter and I wanted to point something out that was dead ahead, I'd say, "It's in my 12 o'clock position" or (for something 90 degrees to the right) "It's at my 3 o'clock" or (for something 90 degrees to the left) "It's at my 9 o'clock." Now, what clock position is the hardest to see? That's right, the one that's behind you, 6 o'clock. When my buddies and I were flying, we had to rely on each other a lot, especially during night weather formation, when our wings overlapped in order to keep the other airplane in sight with lightning all around us. Occasionally, we'd see one of our buddies in the squadron getting a little too cocky, a little too self-assured for his own good and ours. That's when somebody would say, "You'd better check your six. Something's gaining on you and you don't even know it."

Look around you at meetings, sales conferences, and company seminars. Watch for the person who doesn't take notes. There'll be an all-knowing, cocky look, as if to say, "Been there, done that." Do you know what I'd say if I saw that poor, unfortunate, plateaued son of a gun? "You'd better check your six! Something's sneaking up on you and you don't even know it."

Something's coming up your path, and that something is the person or company who's set to outdo you and/or take away your business. When you manage that tricky right turn—the one that leads out of the familiar routine and into new goals and new growth—your client will have better quality work, better customer service, better attention to details. (See illustration 2 in chapter 2.) But what happens if you keep going around and around in the same circle? Plateauing, followed by stagnation, followed by burnout...in that order.

Immediate Action: Think of a person you've worked with who thought he or she knew it all, but didn't. How should he or she have kept up with the challenges of the day? What can you learn from his or her complacency?

Point to Ponder Before You Go On: Don't forget to check your six. You've got to make sure you stay out there where you can focus, for your own good and for the good of others. You've got to make sure that complacency isn't keeping you from developing new talents—and developing defenses against the new challenges you're going to face.

Chapter 10

Break Your
Own Records

*"To be what we are, to become what we are capable of
becoming, is the only end of life."*
—Robert Louis Stevenson

L et's go back to that office of mine and look at what happened
after we got back to the number-one position, but before we
started breaking records.

Once we were there, I went to each one of my salespeople and
told him or her, "I don't want you to worry about breaking anybody
else's sales record. I just want you to worry about breaking your
own—on a daily, weekly, monthly, quarterly, and yearly basis." This
was key to our continued success; they saw immediate positive
results.

I've often heard salespeople say, "I'm going to break so-and-so's
record." That rarely happened. But once I got my people focused on
their own records, breaking them became a piece of cake. They started to see daily progress, then weekly, then monthly, then quarterly,
then yearly. The energy in that office was something to behold and to
be proud of. We broke office records, we broke company records, we
broke industry records. All kinds of articles were written about our
success. The boost was phenomenal—but I always remind myself
that it was all based on getting individual performers to scale new
individual heights.

Immediate Action: Decide what "personal best" record you'll
commit yourself to breaking on a daily, weekly, monthly, quarterly,
and yearly basis. Once you break the first three, the last two are easier!

Point to Ponder Before You Go On: Get specific, in your own
mind, about what continuing at your current level of production will

mean to you. How much will continuing at the current level really cost you? What's the price you're willing to pay to exceed this level? Barriers to your own high performance are generally pushed back only when discomfort with the current situation turns to pain.

Chapter 11

Charlie's Dilemma

"We feel the thing we ought to be beating beneath the thing we are."
—Phillips Brooks, American minister

When I talk about my record-breaking office, I'm often asked, "Where did you find those great salespeople? Did you raid the competition and get their top people? How did you get people who were all cut from the same piece of cloth?" Well, I didn't and they weren't. My salespeople came from every walk of life. That was a great office, and I could tell you some very interesting stories about an entire cross section of people. But I'm just going to pick one. Let's call him Charlie. (That's not his real name.)

Charlie was the most frustrating human being I ever had working for me. If you're a manager, you probably know somebody just like him. I saw potential in him that he refused to see himself because of his self-imposed barriers. This guy made $2,000 a month, month in and month out. I don't even know how he got by on that amount. It was absolutely eerie how close he could get to $2,000 each and every month. It was like an obsession. If he got close to $2,000 and there were just a few days left in the month, he was a basket case. He was actually petrified that someone would walk in and say, "I'm buying from you today," and that would put him over the $2,000.

One month I said to myself, "Charlie doesn't know this yet, but he's going to go through that barrier, or I'm going to die trying to get him over it." I did everything but move in with him. For a solid month, he could not move in that office without my being right behind him. When he went to the men's room, I stood guard at the door! I Big Brothered that son of a gun to death!

That month he made close to $4,000—he doubled his productivity—all thanks to my Big Brothering. But mark the sequel: The next month, without me behind him, Charlie made—you guessed it—

nothing. Zero. And the next month? $2,000—he had no problem with that.

So I brought him in to my office and sat him down. He was one of those people who have "poor me" written all over their faces and in their voices. I bet with that voice of his he could have cracked a Styrofoam cup. Anyway, after I had pointed out what he was doing, he said, "But Danny, you don't understand."

"What don't I understand?" I asked him.

"Well, I've never had any more money in the bank than what my father had in the bank when I was growing up." As ridiculous as that sounds, that was his excuse. He made absolutely sure that he based his earnings solely on what his father used to have when he was young. He controlled his income. If he'd been on salary, he'd have probably controlled it with his expenses. This, then, was his reason for keeping his self-imposed barrier in what could have been a permanent position.

I looked at him and I said, "So that's the role model you're setting for your own children, is it? So someday they'll be able to sit in an office like this and then tell their manager, 'We've never had any more money in the bank than our father had in the bank. It's always been that way in our family.'"

Well, Charlie came up out of that chair in a hurry and headed for my desk, as if I'd not only stepped on sacred ground, I had stomped on it. Or that's the way it seemed. I thought "Cox, here's one you've pushed too far. He's going to be across that desk doing horrible things to your face in just a moment." There he stood at my desk, inches away from me, shaking. But instead of hitting me, he said, "My gosh! That's what I'm doing, isn't it?"

"Sure you are," I said, relieved.

Then he said, "I'm setting a daily example for my kids to see, one of no further growth from their father. My own kids think this is as good as I'll ever be at what I've chosen to do with my life. Well, why should they feel any different? I've never given them any reason to."

He paused a moment, then went on, "They deserve a better example than the one they see at the end of a day when I come home from work, disgusted with myself, carrying the weight of the world on my shoulders, and telling them they'd better get better at what they're doing. From this point forward," Charlie said, "I refuse to continue to repeat what I know doesn't work."

That's an important lesson to learn. When we get into a bad habit, we often don't see what's happening to us and what's not working. But we can defeat that by taking a good, long look at ourselves, and then make changes to break the bad habits—starting today! And that's exactly what Charlie did.

Immediate Action: Ask yourself, "What am I doing now that isn't working? How could I change it?" How do you know whether what you're doing works or not? We probably already know instinctively; the question is, when do we decide that the price we're paying now is too high?

Charlie walked out of my office that day a changed man. Why? Because he had something to prove. The pain of realizing he was affecting his children's life for the worse was too much—he decided it was time to establish a new routine. He vowed to inspire his family. Whom are you inspiring by the way you do your job? (And notice I said "inspiring," not "impressing.")

Point to Ponder Before You Go On: For "things" to change for the better, you've got to change for the better...just as Charlie did.

Chapter 12

Mastering the Right Turn

Two roads diverged in a wood, and I—
I took the one less traveled by,
And that has made all the difference.
—From "The Road Not Taken" by Robert Frost

C harlie's story brings me back to where I started. One of the most important lessons I learned during that time of my life was that every single day we stand at the crossroads of our lives. Every day. Try to envision it once again. As we've seen, a crossroads is really a Y in the road, and every day you stand right at the top, at the fork.

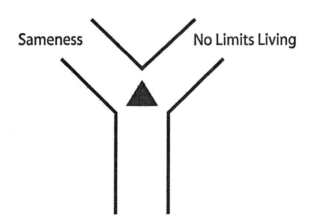

We need to be able to ask ourselves, "Am I doing the best at my job, or am I doing it the way I've always done it?" When you know the answer to that question, then you know where that road leads. More often than not, it leads right back to where you were the day before. Instead of taking that tricky right turn, the one that leads to new growth, you find yourself going around in a very familiar circle.

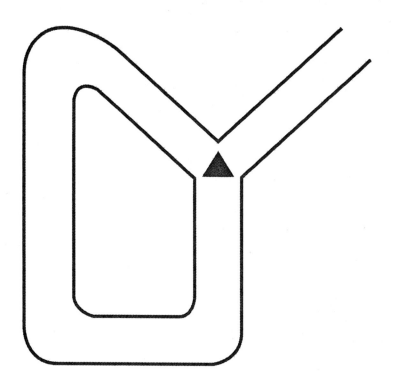

I call that "repeating yesterday." (We'll be examining that idea in more depth later on in this book.) This "repeating yesterday" formula is a phenomenon that's true of companies as well as people—in fact, it would make a pretty good logo for some organizations. These are the companies that I refer to as "Plunging into the future with their eyes affixed to the rear view mirror—they are tradition-centered and unhampered by progress." They don't get worked up about new goals; a fair number of them have no goals whatsoever.

Immediate Action: Make photocopies of this "repeating yester-day" diagram, and place them in strategic locations in your home, your office, and on the dashboard of your car to remind yourself of which way you want to go.

There Are No Limits

Point to Ponder Before You Go On: A love of tradition for its own sake is what I call "nostalgic paralysis"—and it's a sure-fire recipe for stagnation and inefficiency.

Chapter 13

The Right Track

"Short-term comfort for long-term trouble is not the trade you're looking for. The easy way is not the easy way."
—Richard Bach, author

If you're having trouble getting out of bed in the morning, it's because you have no new goals. Every day has become a repeat of the day before. "What's your goal today?" "I'm gonna go in and repeat yesterday." "How was yesterday?" "Not too good." "Then why do it?" "Well, it's my job." Wrong! It's your *habit* in doing your job.

We develop a habit in the way we do the job—then we get bored with the habit and blame our boredom on the job! There's still a lot of adventure and excitement to be realized in your job—if you're willing to work to get better and better at it.

When people quit getting better at what they do, when they stop attaching themselves to constructive goals, it's because there's something inside them that's misleading them into the feeling that they can't get better, no matter what they do, or that they know it all. So they stop taking aim at things. Habit has made them complacent and lazy, a little too self-assured and cocky, like that fighter pilot who forgets to "check his six."

When you're going around in that familiar circle, you're just making a living. When you finally manage that right-hand turn, you could be making a life, with a real sense of enjoyment in what you do—not only something to live on, but something to live for.

I believe that every perceived limitation can be traced to a decision *not* to make that right-hand turn into growth and greatness. In this book, we'll be looking at the best ways to help you manage that turn, day in and day out—and make the right decision at the crossroads.

Immediate Action: Think of the last time you had the opportunity to grow, to stretch yourself, to broaden your abilities—and you took it. Maybe you took a class in a subject you loved, or went "into the zone" to develop a new approach for a problem at work. How did it feel to expand your horizons? Did it leave you feeling more energized, better equipped, and with higher morale to deal with the challenges of life?

Point to Ponder Before You Go On: Will Rogers may have put it best: "Even if you're on the right track, you'll get run over if you just sit there."

Chapter 14

Walking With Giants

"To live is glorious. I have lived!"
—Alice Hubbard (wife of Elbert Hubbard, author of *A Message to Garcia*)

Many, many years ago, my friend and mentor Jim Newton worked very closely with Harvey Firestone. As a matter of fact, his desk was in the same office with Mr. Firestone. Jim was being groomed to take over the company, but instead of following that path, he decided he would go out and do full-time volunteer Christian work. He had what he thought was quite a bit of money. But as it turned out, he and his wife Ellie were in excellent health and lived longer than they planned for. Also, prices went up, and so by 1970 their nest egg was exhausted. They had to start all over again, he at 66 and she at 72.

Jim got tired of trying to live on Social Security. He said, "This isn't working; we can't do this. Let's start a real estate company." Jim had ample experience in this field. As a young man, he'd developed Edison Estates, across from Thomas Edison's home in Florida. So he and his wife started a real estate company. It was very sparse, just a desk and the two of them on a sun porch at a hotel in Fort Myers Beach, Florida. Jim later told me, "We figured we couldn't afford both advertising and a phone, so we opted for advertising—and listed in the ads the number of the pay phone on the wall. We used to pray that no one would be using the phone when a call came in for our office."

Jim and Ellie had 15 real estate offices and close to 200 salespeople when I met them 11 years later. If there is a strong sense of purpose, there is a way of getting things done! Although 1981 was a horrible year in real estate, it was the best year in Jim's company's history up to that point. That's good leadership!

Jim had an uncompromising sense of personal integrity, and he may well be the single most honest man I've ever met. I can't help thinking that those traits have had something to do with his extraordinary life—and the success he built for himself so late in life. He went from trying to live on Social Security to owning a large, and very successful, real estate company, which he eventually sold!

When I first met Jim, he said he was writing a book about Henry Ford, Harvey Firestone, Thomas Edison, Charles Lindbergh, and Dr. Alexis Carrel. (Dr. Carrel invented microsurgery and won the Nobel Prize; he and Lindbergh invented the perfusion pump, which became the heart-lung machine.) I asked him why he had selected those men. "Well," he said, "I was a close personal friend and confidant to all five of them."

The thing that really got my attention was Jim's casual mention that "Lindbergh taught me to fly." I've been around plenty of pilots in my day and have heard a lot of boasting. Most of these boasts were pretty impressive, and some of them were even true—but I've never in my life been as stunned by any pilot's claim as I was when I heard Jim tell me that Lindbergh himself had taught him how to fly!

When he and I first began talking about the book he was writing, Jim was well into his 70s. He asked me what I thought about the project. I told the truth, that I was impressed with his incomparable circle of friends, but that I was a little concerned about trying to reconstitute all the events of the years that had passed. "It's been a long time, Jim," I told him.

"What are you worried about," he countered, "my memory?"

"Honestly, yes," I said.

"Well," he said, "I've got a pretty good memory, and I also have 65 pounds of journals and diaries to back it up."

All of these remarkable men had been Jim's mentors. He had spent an awful lot of time with them. When they would talk about things and share their ideas he would simply take notes. They didn't mind his taking notes and were glad to share their ideas. (Highly creative and productive people are usually very eager to share their ideas.) So he used his voluminous notes to write *Uncommon Friends*, a superb first-hand memoir of life with five of the world's great no-limits achievers.

I had spoken for Jim's company in Florida several times. One of the first times I went down there, he took me out to lunch. At the conclusion of the meal, he said, "I would like to take you over and show

you Mr. Edison's home and Mr. Ford's home here in Fort Myers."
And we were off.

We visited the Edison house. And then he asked the lady he
knew, who had owned Mr. Ford's house ever since the Fords had sold
it, if we could visit the house. (It had been closed to the public for
years, but it is now open for all to enjoy.) She agreed, and we wan-
dered through that remarkable house for quite a while. Jim told me
how he and Mr. Ford would roll back the carpets on weekend nights
for the weekly square dance. Most people don't know that Mr. Ford
loved to call square dances!

After reminiscing about times in the Ford house, Jim and I went
out and sat down on a little retaining wall at the edge of the lawn. The
top was flush with the lawn and at the base was the river that flows
through Fort Myers. We were both in our business suits, sitting there
with our feet dangling over the wall. "I built this wall when I was a
young man," he said. "I built the one next door, behind the Edison
house, first and Mrs. Ford liked it. 'Just bring it on down behind our
house, Jimmy,' she said."

As Jim and I were sitting there on the wall he had built those many years before, I asked, "Jim, is there one particular moment with those great men that's really burned into your mind?"

"Oh, yes," he said, "Mr. Firestone kept an apartment at the Ritz Carlton in New York City. One night, Mr. Ford, Mr. Firestone, and I stood in the bay window of that apartment and looked out the window at the New York skyline and watched as, at exactly 10 p.m., the lights of New York, along with all the other lights in the country, were turned off for two minutes in honor of our friend Thomas Edison. We had attended his funeral that afternoon."

There was a long silence. He was remembering the night he gathered with two friends as they all bid adieu to a beloved mentor. I was coming to terms with the notion that the man who was sitting on this wall with me had once sat in a room with two of America's titans of industry, mourning the passage of the greatest inventor the world had ever known.

"Jim," I said, "You have got to begin your book with that story."

When, some years later, Jim sent me a copy of his book, I opened it up to Chapter One and read the following:

"It is 10 o'clock on the night of October 21st, 1931. The lights are going out all over New York in tribute to the man who lit up the city and much of the world. President Herbert Hoover has asked that lights be dimmed in homes and businesses and on city streets for a couple of minutes to mark the passing of Thomas Edison. Henry Ford, Harvey Firestone, and I stand in silence at a bay window of the Firestone apartment in the old Ritz Carlton looking up Madison Avenue. In one area after another across Manhattan, the Bronx, and beyond, the darkness is spreading...." (From *Uncommon Friends*, by James Newton, Harcourt Brace, 1987.)

I smiled, realizing that, in a small way, thanks to that discussion on the wall my mentor Jim Newton had built, our relationship had been a two-way street. Our time together had helped to shape his book.

Now anyone can go and sit on that wall, perhaps alone, perhaps with a mentor, and share the inspiration of that special place. That's as it should be, I think. Jim has always believed in passing along the spark of inspiration. He received that spark from some of the greatest figures of the 20th century, and has been generous enough to pass along some of what he knows to me. For my part, I hope to share that spark in turn—by sharing the ideas and strategies that show up in the chapters that follow. When your turn to share comes, I hope you'll be as generous to the person who reaches out to you as Jim has been to me.

Immediate Action: Think of at least five people who have had a profound, positive impact in your life. What did you admire most about each of them? What, specifically, did you learn from each?

Point to Ponder Before You Go On: When you run into a person who helps you see your higher self, the self you were meant to be, more clearly—it's in your interest to invest in a relationship with that person.

Chapter 15

Made, Not Born

"The barriers are not yet erected which can say to aspiring talent and industry, 'Thus far and no further.'"
—Ludwig van Beethoven

My friend Jim Newton had worked with—and befriended—some of the greatest minds of the 20th century. Once he and I became close friends, I asked him a question that had been on my mind for some time: What did these no-limits achievers have in common with one another? I learned that there were three fundamental motivations, not only for Jim's five remarkable friends, but also for any number of other barrier-breakers.

I want to share Jim's insights with you on the three driving forces that motivate no-limits achievers, because they're the subject of the next three sections of this book. But before we look at any of that, I want to make a guarantee to you: There is no such thing as a born no-limits performer.

Can you imagine a doctor picking up a newborn baby, showing her off to the assembled nurses, and saying, "Take a look at this young lady—does she look like a superior executive, or what?"

You don't pick up a newspaper and read a birth announcement that says, "A high-performance salesperson was born at St. Joseph's today to John and Mary Smith."

There really is no such thing as a born no-limits person. They build themselves from the ground up. And you can be one of them.

A true story: Harvey Firestone, Thomas Edison, John Burroughs, and Henry Ford stopped at a rural service station on their way to Florida for the winter. (These men loved to travel and camp out together.) "We want some bulbs for our headlights," said Ford. "And by the way, that's Thomas Edison sitting there in the car, and I'm Henry Ford."

The old fellow at the service station didn't even look up; he just spat out some tobacco juice with obvious contempt. "And," said

Ford, "we'd like to buy a new tire—if you have any Firestone tires. That other fellow in the car is Harvey Firestone himself." Still the old fellow said nothing.

While the man was placing the tire on the wheel, the white-bearded John Burroughs—the famous naturalist and author—stuck his head out the window and said, "Howdy, stranger."

The old man at the service station came alive. He glared at Burroughs and said, "If you tell me you're Santa Claus, I'll be danged if I don't crush your skull with this lug wrench."

You never can tell what a no-limits achiever looks or sounds like. And you never can tell about who you may be helping when you help someone!

Immediate Action: Think of a time when you had to develop a new talent or aptitude in order to get by...and you did. Who or what was in charge of that process? Was it "luck" or "fate"—or was it you? I think you'll find it was you!

Point to Ponder Before You Go On: Everything you'll be reading about—all the motivations and traits of no-limits achievers—is attainable for you...once you are willing to commit yourself to the job of becoming the person you were truly meant to be.

Chapter 16

Three Driving Forces

"Restlessness and discontent are the first necessities of progress."
—Thomas Edison

What drives no-limits people? That's what I wanted Jim Newton to reveal. He didn't disappoint me. These high achievers, he explained, are motivated by three *interlocking* and *self-supporting* forces. First of all, no-limits people are inspired by an unshakable sense of purpose. This sense of purpose supports and reinforces (and is supported and reinforced by in turn) two more driving forces. The no-limits person has an unquenchable spirit of adventure and a desire for continued personal growth. These people know they don't know it all. (Anyone who does think he or she knows it all is in what we used to call "the graveyard spiral" in the flying business.)

As I say, these three motivations don't operate in a vacuum. Although the sense of purpose (which is sometimes described as a "sense of mission") initiates the cycle, it connects with each of the other two motivations, and is constantly strengthened by them. Take a look at the diagram on the following page, which I developed after a discussion with Jim. It makes the process a little easier to understand.

The cycle starts in the middle—the no-limits person has developed an incredibly strong sense of "what needs to happen and why." This is the awareness and planning stage, the part of the cycle where goals are developed. Without a firm sense of purpose, without a mission, without a strong goal orientation, there is no such thing as a barrier-breaker.

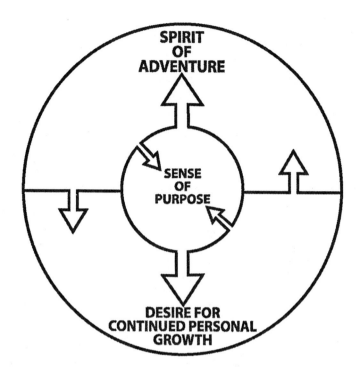

So the goal's established and a plan is in place. Then the no-limits person launches that plan and embarks on the adventure of actually achieving the goal. Of course, there are challenges and temporary setbacks along the way; problem-solving is part of the adventure. This is the second phase of the process, and it's very exciting.

Even after the goal is achieved, the no-limits person is motivated—this time, to prepare for the challenges of the future. That third element, the desire for continued personal growth, is a commitment not to "rest on laurels" or "stick with the formula" because it's always worked before. No-limits people are about positive change, positive growth, and forward movement. For them, the cycle is not complete until there's evidence of renewal and new understanding.

All three motivations support and reinforce one another. All three are essential forces for the development of a no-limits life.

This book is divided into four sections. The first one, which you've almost completed, talks about what no-limits people, barrier-breakers, look like. The next three focus in detail on the specifics of the three-part process we've just examined: the sense of purpose, the spirit of adventure, and the desire for continued personal growth.

These are the driving forces that no-limits people use to put their lives into "afterburner" mode, to use Air Force terminology. With practice, you can use these forces to change your life, too!

Immediate Action: Review the three forces that drive no-limits achievers. Jot them down on a separate sheet of paper.

Point to Ponder Before You Go On: No-limits people are those who commit to pushing themselves outside of the comfort zone, those who know what they want and are willing to commit fully to the adventure of achieving their goals, and those who are willing to say, as my friend Jim Rohn says, "In order to do more, I've got to be more."

Chapter 17

The Peaks
and the Pits

"The world is a grindstone. Life's your nose."
—Fred Allen, humorist

In this life, we usually don't stand still for long. We all have goals, and we all have role models. It's just a question of whether those role models are positive or negative. We're either moving upward, toward the peak, toward constructive, life-affirming goals-thanks to the influence of positive role models—or we're moving downward, toward the pits, toward inauthentic, life-destroying goals—thanks to the influence of negative role models.

Choosing between those two options is like flying a plane. If we surround ourselves with the right mentors, we start a climb into the stratosphere. If we spend too much time on the negative side, we lose our altitude—and run the risk of crashing. And that can ruin your whole day!

Pilots don't have to be told that. All the same we have a reminder that we use in the skies—I call it the ABC principle. This is a complex, technical guideline that has some important applications in the world nonfliers occupy, too. The ABC principle states that

Anything's
Better than
Crashing!

Anything—you name it, anything—beats crashing. That's true when you're flying faster than the speed of sound, of course, but it's also true of the life we choose for ourselves. Talented people such as Ernest Hemingway, Lenny Bruce, Janis Joplin, Jim Morrison, and John Belushi all made the wrong "altitude" choices. They began to plunge downward, and they crashed. They're not around anymore, because they picked the wrong role models and embraced the wrong values. They climbed in the cockpit, fired up the engine, hit the skies, and then picked up speed at the worst possible moment: while they were heading toward hard real estate. No matter how impressive their accomplishments may have been before that plunge, their examples are not a recipe for success, or even survival. They're a recipe for disaster.

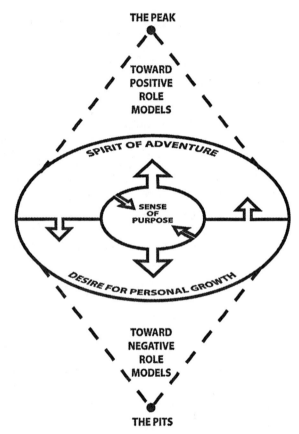

Immediate Action: Who's the best example of a person you've met or know about who's headed for the peak, not the pits? What can you learn from that person? List those points.

Point to Ponder Before You Go On: Each of us has the choice to climb toward the stars...or point ourselves toward something that's going to end with us eating a whole lot of gravel. The stars are more fun to look at and they're easier on your face than the gravel.

Chapter 18

Crystal-clear Focus
on the Future

"People are afraid of the future, of the unknown. If a man faces up to it and takes the dare of the future, he can have some control over his destiny. That's an exciting idea to me, better than waiting with everybody else to see what's going to happen."
—John H. Glenn, Jr.

Here's another important thing I learned from Jim Newton: No-limits people focus with the intensity of a laser beam on *what's still possible.* Once they commit themselves to a goal—and to the ongoing development of their own talents and abilities—they don't spend a whole lot of time looking back and wondering how things might have turned out. They make their own luck. They don't get sidetracked worrying about what's gone wrong in the past; they study what works, identify exactly what doesn't, and then move forward.

No-limits people, in other words, learn to focus instinctively on what will still be. Most other people, by contrast, have taught themselves to focus instinctively on what might have been.

Take a look at the chart on the following page, which illustrates the difference between "might-have-been" thinking and "will-still-be" thinking.

Look around you, and you'll find that most people are content simply to get through the day. They focus on "bad luck" or "rotten breaks" and look for excuses not to perform at peak levels. Of course, they usually find those excuses. If there were any honesty in the world, the majority of people would plan their days in daily planners that would have a long list of "opportunities to give in today" and perhaps one line devoted to a *possible* success!

	Might have been	Will still be
Growth	None	Daily, because of commitment made
Goals	None significant	Constantly achieving daily goals
Friends	Same demeanor	Expanding circle of inspiring people
Learning source	TV	Books, tapes, friends
Direction	Backward	Forward
Objective	Get through day	Contribute to day
Outlook	Bleak	Bright

The way people think about the day ahead—"It'll never work! We're doomed!" or "God never gives me more than I can handle. I know I can learn from whatever I encounter today"—has a profound impact on the amount we achieve. If we ask merely to get through the day, that's what we'll achieve! If we focus on "what might have been," we never give ourselves the opportunity to become excited about "what will be!"

Immediate Action: Think of someone you know or have worked with whose habits and attitudes remind you of those of the "might-have-been" thinker. Now think of someone you know or have worked with whose example is closer to that of the "will-still-be" thinker. Whose life is more exciting? Whose rewards are more inspiring? Whose company do you enjoy more?

Point to Ponder Before You Go On: No-limits people fall into my category of "accelerationists," because they ACCELERATE! Here's what I mean by that:

A—Awareness. They're aware of the current situation and the goals they've set.

C—Commitment. They're committed to developing their strengths.

C—Celebrate. They celebrate goals and achievement on a daily basis.

E—Education. They view this as a neverending process.

L—Laughter. They know how to laugh, and they do it often! (Laughter gets rid of negative stress.)

E—Energize. Their energy rubs off on others.

R—Responsibility. They encourage team accountability and are willing to stand behind their own decisions.

A—Aim. They keep raising it.

T—Time. They take time for themselves and for their family.

E—Evaluate. They regularly evaluate what's happened and why. In other words, they learn from themselves, as well as others.

Chapter 19

Characteristics That Barrier-breakers Cultivate

"There are three types of people in this world—the 'wills,' the 'won'ts,' and the 'can'ts.' The first accomplish everything, the second oppose everything, the third fail in everything."
—Anonymous

Barrier-breakers are people who are purposeful, who embrace adventure, and who keep forcing themselves out of their established comfort zones and into zones of high achievement. They're the people who learn how to overcome the deadening force of habit and routine in their lives, people who transcend "good enough" and learn how to demand the best from themselves on a regular basis. For these folks, there are no limits to self-improvement and no limits to what they can achieve.

Last year, I was lucky enough to meet one of the truly great barrier-breakers of all time, Neil Armstrong, command pilot of Apollo 11 and the first man to walk on the moon, when the Lindbergh Foundation presented him with its Lindbergh Award. The award is given each year to one individual whose lifelong contributions have exhibited great technological strides, while doing no harm to nature. (Lindbergh's lifelong love affair with nature and his passion for environmental preservation are important parts of his legacy that are often forgotten.) The ceremony took place that year at the Air Force Academy in Colorado Springs, Colorado.

Following the presentation, my wife and I made our way forward to meet Armstrong. He was pleasant, approachable, and extremely engaging. Shaking his hand has to rank as one of the great honors of my life. I asked if he was familiar with the airplane in which I had spent some 1,200 hours of my life, the F-101B "Voodoo." When I mentioned the plane to him, Armstrong's face lit up. "Oh, yes," he said, "I did pitch up tests on it, and I also helped to develop the equipment and procedures for handling that problem."

A "pitch up" is a technical term for something pilots of this particular airplane, as a rule, avoid at all costs. Because of the aerodynamic structure of the airplane, it could tumble right out of the sky! It's a great way to get your adrenaline pumping. If you're ever feeling lackadaisical, pitching up is a great way to focus your attention on the situation at hand. I had an F-101 pitch up once and only once in my flying career, and I knew full well the moment it happened that I was definitely experiencing something I hadn't asked for. When the tumbling was over, I was 30,000 feet closer to the ground than I had been. I remember thinking to myself—calmly and objectively, of course—that one episode of losing control of my plane and plunging toward the real estate I was used to soaring over was quite enough for me. That experience was the ninth pitch up the Air Force had had with that kind of airplane, and only three pilots ahead of me had survived!

And here was Neil Armstrong telling me—with a nostalgic smile on his face—that he'd done this on a daily basis! I was impressed that he had been the first man on the moon, but I was more impressed that he'd done pitch ups on purpose! Had he not done those tests, far more pitch ups would have occurred—and many more fatalities.

Talk about pushing yourself out of the comfort zone! The story proves that Armstrong was a barrier-breaker long before his trip to the moon, a fact that shouldn't come as much of a surprise to anyone. I think Armstrong's personal history, his character, and his attitude toward both his work and his place in history also show that he shares important habits with "no-limits" performers from all walks of life.

I've been lucky enough to work with many kinds of barrier-breakers. In addition to being motivated by the three forces Jim Newton identified, I believe they all share, with Armstrong, 10 characteristics, developed on purpose. Here they are:

Characteristic #1: Barrier-breakers possess uncompromising integrity. Back home, we have a saying about someone you can't trust: "He's so crooked, he could hide behind a corkscrew." Nobody says that about barrier-breakers. They don't cut corners. During good times and lean times, the barrier-breaker's values remain the same. They don't violate their own ethical standards for short-term gain (or long-term gain, for that matter). When you're a barrier-breaker, you know full well that you can wash your hands, but you can't wash your conscience. At the end of the day, you don't lose sleep over the tough decisions, because you know you've made them in accordance with your conscience.

Characteristic #2: Barrier-breakers develop and maintain extremely high personal energy levels. Part of this is because they refuse to devote attention to things that are merely interesting, rather than things that are important. (They know that not everything that's interesting is important!) Barrier-breakers know that the habit of controlling what you pay attention to is essential to maintaining a high personal energy level. They focus on people and things that energize them and they usually energize others in the process. (See Characteristic #8.) You don't find barrier-breakers who look like they were "born tired and then had a relapse." By the way, barrier-breakers also refuse to get involved in anything that's petty. That's the greatest drain of energy you can have in your life or in your company.

Characteristic #3: Barrier-breakers are good at working priorities. That's another way of saying they don't get sidetracked by momentary challenges that don't carry much real significance, and they don't put off little problems that carry big implications. My motto on this score comes from my early years in Southern Illinois, where people used to tell me, "If you've got a frog to swallow, don't look at it too long. If you've got more than one to swallow, swallow the biggest one first." (And as someone in one of my recent seminars said, "They taste better fresh!") Barrier-breakers know they've got to tend to the frogs that do show up on their desks, and tend to the big ones first, day in and day out. After all, leaving a frog unswallowed for an extended period may mean walking into your office to find a frog the size of a Chrysler sitting on your desk! I'll tell you something else interesting about barrier-breakers: They don't have any number-two priorities. That's right. When they wrap up work on their no-doubt-about-it number-one priority, they treat the next item on the list as what it is: the new number-one priority. Then they repeat the process. Because they always swallow the big frogs first, barrier-breakers don't expend a great deal of time and energy on trivial things. They do spend a great deal of time tackling the issues that really matter. They make a habit of this, and as a result they get to be quite good at what they do. They're very stable under pressure, and they're excellent problem-solvers.

Characteristic #4: Barrier-breakers are courageous. They understand that either they are in charge of a given moment in time or fear is. Barrier-breakers don't let fear dictate the agenda. They're not "safe plodders," and they don't waste a lot of their time fantasizing about the awful things that might happen to them. They know that life is a series of risks—and that avoiding each one of those risks is pretty much impossible. Barrier-breakers also know that people who try to reduce every element of risk from their lives are like the fellow who wouldn't take his car out of the parking lot until he could see all the traffic lights on Main Street turn green at the same time! Too many people spend their lives driving around life's parking lot. They're in motion, but not in direction. Keep asking yourself, "Am I in motion today, or am I in direction?"

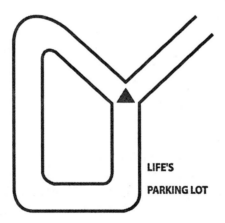

LIFE'S
PARKING LOT

Characteristic #5: Barrier-breakers are truly committed and dedicated hard workers. They need no supervising, and they are masters at motivating themselves. Barrier-breakers do what they love, and they love what they do, so it's really no problem for them to channel all their energy into the worthy objectives they set for themselves. When people compliment barrier-breakers on how committed they are, how hard they work, the recipients of these compliments are often a little bit taken aback. They're already doing what they were meant to do! The outside world may look at that as "working hard," but they don't. They just keep on charging ahead. (A successful woman I worked with a while back described herself this way: "God didn't make me with an 'off switch!'")

Characteristic #6: Barrier-breakers are a bit unorthodox. They don't worry about the consequences of not looking, sounding, or acting like other people. They aren't afraid to try new approaches and challenge the established routine. They may get the wind knocked out of them every once in a while for their troubles, but they hardly ever make the same mistakes twice. They learn from their unorthodoxy, because they know, as Tess Cowper put it, that "ignorance is an expensive university, and fools are not educated cheaply." Barrier-breakers love to make things interesting, even if it means making the occasional mistake—and they learn as they go along, without rerunning those mistakes.

Characteristic #7: Barrier-breakers are goal-oriented. They don't bounce through the day like a Ping-Pong ball; they take clear steps that are meant to bring them closer to a particular, predetermined goal. They measure their every act against the goal that makes the most sense for them, and they're willing to face adversity for a time to achieve that goal. I once asked former heavyweight champ George Foreman how he managed to stand fast during the savage punches opponents would launch against him in the ring. (I asked this after noticing the condition of the great boxer's nose, which must be one of the world's great monuments to goal orientation.) Foreman told me, "If I see what I want real good in my mind, I don't notice any pain in getting it." If there's better, more concise advice on the art of staying goal-oriented, I haven't come across it yet. If you're experiencing pain in getting what you want, it's because you aren't seeing what you want "real good" in your mind.

Characteristic #8: Barrier-breakers have an inspired enthusiasm that's contagious. Can you think of someone you've lived with or worked with who "turned on" a room the minute he or she walked into it? Someone who made everyone feel better about whatever was on the agenda? Someone who helped you to focus on the positive, time after time? That's contagious enthusiasm, and barrier-breakers are masters at spreading it around. They know that everything they do—positively or negatively—affects the world around them, and they choose to affect the world positively, even when times are tough. They've developed this in-depth enthusiasm by witnessing the accomplishment of their daily goals, which are part of a larger plan. Barrier-breakers realize the wisdom of Eden Philpott's observation that the world we live in is "full of magical things patiently waiting for our wits to grow sharper." They're always on the lookout for newer and more magical things, and they delight in sharing their excitement about those things with other people.

Characteristic #9: Barrier-breakers are level-headed. You can hardly ever spook barrier-breakers. They aren't easily distracted; you won't find them pretending to know something they don't. They grasp new facts quickly and easily. Barrier-breakers are supremely poised, even in situations that others would find daunting or confusing. Barrier-breakers have a knack for bringing a sense of order to the most turbulent situations. Neil Armstrong's work inducing pitch up in the F-101B is a pretty fair example of just how much poise some barrier-breakers can summon!

Characteristic #10: Barrier-breakers want to help others grow. They know that there's nothing to be gained by talking down the dreams of other people. Barrier-breakers support the aspirations of others. They know that excessive political gamesmanship is a waste of time and energy, and they don't invent new enemies whenever there's a shortage of old ones. Barrier-breakers are eager to support (and credit) the new plans and ideas of others.

Immediate Action: Take a few moments to give yourself a rating, on a 1-to-10 scale, in each of the 10 characteristics common to barrier-breakers. Honestly, would a colleague, close friend, or family member rate you the same in these 10 areas? If your numbers are higher than the numbers someone else assigns you (and they probably will be), consider the high numbers you gave yourself to be your target figures—the numbers you should be shooting for—and the lower numbers to be where you are right now.

Point to Ponder Before You Go On: Reread Characteristic #8. Then think about this: If you don't have that inspired enthusiasm that's contagious, then whatever you do have is also contagious.

Chapter 20

Guiding Voices: Breaking Barriers

Here are some observations from Master Teachers on the subject of breaking barriers.

"The faster I got, the smoother the ride. Suddenly the Mach needle began to fluctuate. It went up to .965 Mach—then tipped right off the scale. After all the anxiety, after all the anticipation, breaking the sound barrier, the unknown, was just a poke through Jell-O, a perfectly paved speedway, because the real barrier wasn't in the sky, but in our knowledge and experience of supersonic flight."
—From pilot Chuck Yeager's autobiography, *Yeager*

"The only way to discover the limits of the possible is to go beyond them, to the impossible."
—Arthur C. Clarke

"I'm looking for a lot of [people] who have an infinite capacity to not know what can't be done."
—Henry Ford

"If we all did the things we are capable of doing, we would literally astound ourselves."
—Thomas Edison

"The brain's capacity is almost inexhaustible."
—Dr. Irwin Ross, researcher

"Impossible? That is not good French."
—Napoleon

Danny Cox

"One of the great discoveries a man makes, one of his great surprises, is to find he can do what he was afraid he couldn't do."
—Henry Ford

"Audacity is one of man's most precious qualities. If he lacks that, he'll never amount to anything."
—Dr. Alexis Carrel, French surgeon and Nobelist

"I feel like my greatest work is still out in front of me."
—Jim Newton, in his mid-80s.

"It is the youngest age I have left."
—The Roman statesman Cato, in response to friends who marveled at his decision to begin studying Greek at the age of 80.

"Thank you, God, for everything. If I didn't accept all the good things you offered, it wasn't your fault; they were there. I'll be around tomorrow."
—Writer Marie Beatty's bedtime prayer

"We want it all. From the instant we saw the birds flying, we wanted what the birds had. It's intensely human to want it all. That's how we recognize thresholds. They show us what we don't have. We took what the birds had, but now we want the stars and every planet we've ever imagined...and the ones yet to be imagined. Thus, there will always be thresholds. We ask only the right to cross them."
—From *Threshold: The Blue Angels Experience*, by Frank Herbert

"An idea that is not dangerous is unworthy to be called an idea at all."
—Elbert Hubbard

"Knowledge fosters criticism and doubt. But the man who has no criticisms, has no mind. And the man who ceases to ask questions, ceases to exist."
—Alan Ashley-Pitt, writer

"Every great scientific truth goes through three stages. First, people say it conflicts with the Bible. Next, they say it has been discovered before. Lastly, they say they have always believed it."
—Jean Louis Agassiz, naturalist, geologist, and educator

"Resolve to take Fate by the throat and shake a living out of her."
—Louisa May Alcott

"Reputation is what you're supposed to be; character is what you are."
—William Hersey Davis, author

"I am of the opinion that my life belongs to the whole community and, as long as I live, it is my privilege to do for it whatever I can. I want to be thoroughly used up when I die. For the harder I work, the more I live. I rejoice in life for its own sake. Life is no brief candle to me. It's a sort of splendid torch which I've got to hold up for the moment and I want to make it burn as brightly as possible before handing it on to future generations."
—George Bernard Shaw

"Everything comes to him who waits—provided he hustles while he waits."
—Thomas Edison's inscription on a picture of himself that he gave to Jim Newton

"A wish is a goal without any action attached to it."
—Anonymous

"Luck: Laboring Under Correct Knowledge."
—Denis Waitley, author and speaker

"Energy is another name for enthusiasm."
—Orison Swett Marden

"Success is perseverance applied to a practical end."
—Alexander Graham Bell

"A cheerful disposition is a fund of ready capital, a magnet for the good things of life."
—Orison Swett Marden

"Last Sunday, a young man died here of extreme old age at 25."
—Jim Newton

"We can achieve what we can conceive."
—Elbert Hubbard

"Enjoying one's work as art.
"Transcending previous performances.
"Never becoming too comfortable.
"Rehearsing things mentally beforehand.
"Not focusing too much on questions of blame and where it should be placed."
—Dr. Charles Garfield's hallmarks of top performers

"It must be borne in mind that the tragedy of life does not lie in not reaching your goals; the tragedy lies in not having any goals to reach. It isn't a calamity to die with dreams unfulfilled, but it is a calamity not to dream. It is not a disaster to be unable to capture your ideals, but it is a disaster to have no ideals to capture. It is not a disgrace not to reach the stars, but it is a disgrace to have no stars to reach."
—Dr. Benjamin Isaiah Mays, writer

"His mind is addled; he's not worth keeping in school any longer."
—Eight-year-old Thomas Edison's grade-school teacher

"I never did a day's work in my life. It was all fun."
—Thomas Edison

"The day before the funeral."
—Edison's response to the question "When will you retire?"

"If one stands up and is counted from time to time, one may get knocked down. But remember this: A man flattened by an opponent

can get up again. A man flattened by conformity stays down for good. Follow the path of the unsafe, independent thinker. Expose your ideas to the dangers of controversy. Speak your mind and fear less the label of 'crackpot' than the stigma of conformity. And on issues that seem important, stand up and be counted at any cost."
—Thomas J. Watson, business executive and first president of IBM

"A five-year study of 120 of the nation's top artists, athletes, and scholars has concluded that drive and determination, not great natural talent, led to their extraordinary success.

"'We expected to find tales of great natural gifts,' said University of Chicago education professor Benjamin Bloom....'We didn't find that at all. Their mothers often said it was their other child who had the greater gift....'

"The most brilliant mathematicians often said they had trouble in school and were rarely the best in their classes. Some world-class tennis players said their coaches viewed them as being too short ever to be outstanding, and the Olympic swimmers said they remember getting regularly 'clobbered' in races as 10-year-olds....

"(T)he researchers heard accounts of an extraordinary drive and dedication through which, for example, a child would practice the piano several hours daily for 17 years to attain his goal of becoming a concert pianist. A typical swimmer would tell of getting up at 5:30 every morning to swim two hours before school and then two hours after school to attain his or her goal of making the Olympic team."
—From the *Los Angeles Times,* February 7, 1985

"Any fool can count the seeds in an apple, but only God can count the apples in a seed."
—Ancient proverb

"My message to you is: Be courageous! I have lived a long time. I have seen history repeat itself again and again. I have seen many depressions in business. Always America has come out stronger and more prosperous. Be as brave as your fathers before you. Have faith! Go forward!"
—Thomas Edison's final public message, delivered during the depths of the Great Depression

"Tough times never last but tough people do."
—Dr. Robert H. Schuller, "Hour of Power" minister

"He lives best and most who gives God his greatest opportunity in him."
—Anonymous

"Failure is only the opportunity to more intelligently begin again."
—Henry Ford

"I would be the least among men with dreams and the desire to fulfill them, rather than the greatest with no dreams and no desires."
—Kahlil Gibran

"Imagination is more important than knowledge."
—Albert Einstein

"Argue for your limitations and you get to keep them."
—Richard Bach, author

"Compared to what we ought to be, we are only half-awake."
—William James, philosopher and psychologist

"I know there is infinity beyond ourselves. I wonder if there is infinity within."
—Charles Lindbergh (This is one of his last written notes. It was found on a nightstand next to his deathbed.)

"I know this world is ruled by infinite intelligence."
—Thomas Edison

Part 2:

Your Driving Purpose

Chapter 21

The Moment
of Truth

"Getting to the point of deciding is the hard part. Once you're there, it's simple. I call it 'reaching the core'....Whatever the words, I'm sure this reality is the force at the heart of the universe. That force becomes available to us in some measure."
—Charles Lindbergh

Have you ever had an experience that changed the way you looked at your life? In the final pages of his book *Walden,* Henry David Thoreau wrote about the importance of living in the direction of one's own highest and best aspirations—of realizing one's own true purpose in life. He wrote about his decision to live in the wilderness for a time and about what he had learned from that decision:

"The surface of the earth...is soft and impressible by the feet of men; and so with the paths which the mind travels. How worn and dusty, then, must be the highways of the world— how deep the ruts of tradition and conformity!...I learned this, at least, by my experiment: that if one advances confidently in the direction of his dreams, he will meet with a success unexpected in common hours. He will put some things behind, will pass an invisible boundary; new, universal, and more liberal laws will begin to establish themselves around and within him; or the old laws will be expanded and interpreted in his favor in a more liberal sense and he will live with the license of a higher order of beings."

Thoreau, in writing that passage, was describing, not his political leanings, but what I call a "moment of truth."

There Are No Limits

High achievement—no-limits achievement—begins first in the mind. So does low achievement. Low achievement is easy; we've got no shortage of examples to follow in that area. High achievement requires energy—it asks us to break free of the "ruts of tradition and conformity" when the situation demands that we do so—and it often does! Some folks follow old wagon tracks. Others blaze new trails. Blazing trails takes a little more gumption. As we said in the fighter squadrons, "No guts, no air medals."

We each make the choices that support either high achievement or low achievement on a daily basis. Those choices establish the plans (formal or informal) that we set up for our lives. We each decide whether we're going to move forward, into uncharted territory that may carry a few risks...or avoid taking on new challenges and stick with what's already familiar to us.

The moment of truth is the moment when we decide either to continue with the predictable, numbing routines of the past or to make a habit of experiencing something new, to follow a path that demands the most from us (and offers us the most satisfying rewards). The moment of truth is the point when we are faced with the choice of either succumbing to the habits we have followed before or establishing a new and driving purpose in our lives. That purpose is a force strong enough to help us move out of the "ruts of tradition and conformity." It only comes to our aid when we decide for ourselves that the old way of doing things no longer makes sense.

Is there a sadder reason to take on any task than "that's the way we've always done it"? When we break through the habit of doing things as they've always been done, then we're making the most of our moment of truth. I believe that success is the result of a (sometimes sudden) direction-changing decision that rejects old preconceptions, and is followed by a long period of slow growth and hard work. But the decision to take on a new challenge must come first! In moments of truth, we decide. We see who we really are and what we're really here for, and we stop making excuses.

Often, people say they're limited by parents, a difficult childhood, the environment, a spouse, a bad boss, or any number of other factors. The truth is, though, that we make the decisions that allow unfortunate influences to affect us positively or negatively. When we choose to accept (and reinforce!) those negative influences, we step away from no-limits thinking. When we take personal responsibility for every moment we are given from this moment onward, we're making the very most of our lives and strengthening our personal sense of purpose—the first of the driving forces that motivates no-limits achievers.

These achievers know that every thought is a seed that produces a mental plant exactly like itself—and the key word here is "exactly." Once we see vividly the folly of using our minds to plant only "seeds for weeds," then we're experiencing our moment of truth.

I believe that we all have the tools required to complete the job that fulfills our destiny, and that chief among these tools is the mind itself. All we have to do is keep the tools sharp and get at the work that must be accomplished. The decision to do this, no matter what, is the moment of truth.

In this second section of this book, you'll be learning more about the development of the sense of purpose, that first driving force that makes barrier-breaker achievement possible. With just a little practice, you'll learn to instill this driving sense of purpose in your life—by setting goals that make sense for you, inspire you, and get your heart pumping. Like barrier-breakers everywhere, you will learn to ask yourself questions that get you motivated:

- Why am I here? (What difference do I want to make to my company, my family, my community, my country?)

- What goal is most important to me? (Launching a new company? Developing a new proposal that will help my company achieve a major objective and help me grow? Finding a new job that makes full use of my talents?)

- What is the person I *could* be capable of becoming? (Make a habit of asking yourself, "Which direction does my life need to face, and what's the very first step?")

- Am I receiving $40,000 per year for potential that could bring me $100,000 or more per year? (Is working within a tradition-bound culture robbing me of opportunity and growth?)

- Am I paying too much to be supervised? (If I'm capable of generating $100,000 in revenue, and I'm being paid $40,000, then I'm paying $60,000 for the privilege of being managed by someone!)

- How can I picture myself only as I want to become today, and thus build a "self-fulfilling prophecy"? (How specific can I make the picture?)

- Am I measuring myself by what I have done, what I will do, or what I am capable of doing? (Barrier-breakers focus on what they're capable of doing!)

- What am I currently doing out of sheer force of habit that *isn't* working? (What could I be doing instead?)

That last question is a particularly important one. Doing away with the unnecessary and the inefficient is one of the most important steps to a high-performance, barrier-breaker life style. Most people find ways, though, to repeat what they know full well doesn't work, or at least doesn't work well. Barrier-breakers, on the other hand, know that holding on to what doesn't work is a formula for mediocrity—or worse. They know, because they've experienced a moment of truth, and they've decided not to accept anything less than the best from themselves.

But you can't summon the first of the three forces behind a no-limits life style—the driving sense of purpose—without a "moment of truth," a moment when you decide, with a burning conviction, to devote your life to taking that ever-present right-hand turn out of inefficient, unproductive habit and into new areas of achievement. (See the diagram on page 47.)

The moment of truth is the moment when you accept full responsibility for your own life, your own experiences, and your own decisions, and commit yourself to the task of accomplishing all that the person you *could* be *could* accomplish. It's the moment when you commit yourself to being the person you deserve to be and to setting the goals that that person has a right to achieve.

One of my favorite writers, Orison Swett Marden, who wrote at the turn of the 20th century, would probably ask a very simple question about each person's moment of truth. He'd want to know whether it identified your "North Star" course, the uniquely true and constant direction of your life.

"In a factory where mariners' compasses are made," Marden wrote, "before the needles are magnetized, they will lie in any position—but once touched by the mighty magnet, once electrified by that mysterious power, they ever afterwards point only in one direction. Many a young life lies listless, purposeless, until touched by the Divine Magnet, after which, if it nourishes its aspirations, it always points to the North Star of its hope and its ideal."

When you experience a moment of truth, you are identifying your own North Star, picking out the unchanging vision that you will use to establish all your goals. We need to use that North Star course to test each goal. We need to be able to ask, "Is this goal aiming in the direction of my vision? Is it pointing me where I eventually want to go?" The star won't get us there by itself, but at least it should be able to help us find out when we're taking a step in the right direction.

Accomplishment is your birthright. Limitations are adopted. Your own moment of truth can take place at the instant you vow, at a deep and unrevokable level, to take appropriate action to bring about a new life and to work to transcend the (perceived) limitations that are keeping you from attaining your highest aspirations.

Your moment of truth is the moment when you promise to hold nothing back. It's the moment you acknowledge that, from this point forward, you yourself are worth your own supreme effort.

Immediate Action: One of my mentors had me do the following exercise: Take a pen and paper and describe who you are in three sentences. This is a harder task than it sounds! It will give you an idea of what's important to you, how you view yourself, and what your guiding values are. Focus on the positive—frame your description in terms of what you're capable of doing, not the points where you feel you've come up short in life.

Here's my own answer to the "Who am I?" question. Come up with your own three-sentence answer, one that will help you spark your own moment of truth!

- I am a growing person.
- I've been put on this earth, not to keep it the same, but to make it better.
- I have the ability to influence others by the spoken and written word, a responsibility I do not take lightly.

There Are No Limits

Taking the time to define yourself in positive terms will help you get a fix on the person you're meant to be. This self-assessment—a critical component of the moments of truth that inspire no-limits achievers and initiate a firm sense of purpose—is a habit never developed by mediocre performers. (Back home, we used to say that there are some folks who never manage to make a name for themselves anywhere except on a tombstone.)

Point to Ponder Before You Go On: The person who can't make a choice, has made a choice. The person who discovers his or her own true purpose is in the perfect position to select the right goals...and to make only the choices that support those goals.

Chapter 22

"In Direction"

"I find the great thing in this world is not so much where we stand, as in what direction we are moving."
—Oliver Wendell Holmes

Think about the direction of your life, the reason you're here. Ask yourself some tough questions about why, exactly, you get up every morning.

Is your "best yet to be"? Does the high point of your life seem to lie in your past, or is it in your future?

Are you "in direction" toward that high point, or do you often find that you are "in motion" toward the low-end goal of getting through the day?

Does your life have a sense of purpose about it, or are there days when you feel as though you're working at full speed, and with full intensity, simply to stay in the same place?

Life is a constant battle between the inertia of failure and the inertia of success. The inertia of failure is stagnation, boredom, lost opportunity, and undeveloped or "hidden" potential. For my money, I think the only potential that counts is the potential that is brought into existence. It's pretty hard to tell the difference between a "hidden ability" to perform well and an "obvious ability" to perform poorly. The inertia of success, on the other hand, is movement, excitement, development, and the eradication of (perceived) barriers to achievement.

Listen. Can you hear a long, high-pitched beep coming from somewhere? I can. This life we are living is not a test of the Emergency Broadcast System. It is our actual, real life, and we have all been instructed to tune in to our own highest aspirations for instructions and official information on how best to live it.

We know when our life began: the day we were born. But when will our living begin? And if it doesn't begin right here, and right now, when will it? What action will we take to bring that living about? Not only are we the architects of our own fates, we've got to lay the bricks, as well! Each of us must ask: Are we willing to treat our life as the "real thing"—our journey toward the high point we deserve to reach—and not as a test?

Immediate Action: Ask yourself, "What one thing can I do thoroughly, with proficiency, that moves me toward an important goal— what one thing?" That's the activity to focus on!

Point to Ponder Before You Go On: Once you truly know your direction, failure is virtually impossible. It will only come about when you yourself concede defeat...and when you yourself give up any effort to learn from what you've experienced. This doesn't mean, however, that you won't run into some real challenges along the new road.

Chapter 23

Destiny Goals

"Make no little plans; they have no magic to stir men's blood, and probably they will not be realized. Make big plans; aim high in hope and work, remembering that a noble, logical diagram once recorded will never die, but long after we are gone will be a living thing, asserting itself with ever-growing insistency."
—Daniel Burnham, British architect

Your goals should be big enough, bold enough, and exciting enough, to turn you on. If they are, and if your goals point you in the right direction, you'll notice that some strange things will start to happen. You'll start to get excited about taking your goals on, you'll start to get better at what you do, and doors will start opening up for you.

Out of constructive goal orientation springs self-discipline, and from self-discipline comes a personal freedom centered around high achievement. This process of choosing worthy goals and dedicating yourself to them completely is pretty much identical to the process of developing that old-fashioned, and timeless, virtue known as "good character."

It's not a lack of talent, but a lack of goals, that causes one's life to stagnate. As our daily goals, our commitment to fulfill them, and our confidence in our own ability to fulfill them all increase, our future life style improves. As we believe more deeply in our goals, we believe more deeply in ourselves, and life gets better.

The size of our past goals has determined our present life style. The size of our future goals will determine our future life style. It's as simple as that. Simple but not easy. I won't kid you about the hard work that's required. But as George Foreman said in Chapter 19, "If I see what I want real good in my mind, I don't notice any _____ in getting it." (How would you fill in the blank?)

When we make a commitment to accomplishment—not to waiting passively for change, but to making change happen through organized planning—the resulting improvement in morale becomes a vote of confidence for our life. In fact, I think this improvement in morale is the difference between real life and simple existence. We benefit not only from the achievement itself, but from an upward surge in morale. That's why I believe that the very first step in morale-building has to be the development of a plan that excites and motivates.

A goal's main purpose is to help develop undeveloped potential. The goal motivates us to action. We work hard and overcome obstacles, and the achieved goal becomes a reward for the effort extended and the growth realized. There's a wonderful boost in morale, and the cycle begins again. Fortunately, we don't have to look far for the "fuel" that moves this cycle forward.

Constructive goals are not limiting; they're liberating. Only goals that point you toward unhealthy or unethical outcomes are exhausting. Unfortunately, many people spend large chunks of their lives pursuing these negative objectives.

Experiencing temporary setbacks is not a crime. Low aim is! So, what are you aiming for? Your goals should make sense for where you've been, where you are now, and where you're headed. A person without constructive goals is truly blinded, because he or she can't see the best possible future!

Be sure you set goals that are:
1. Exciting.
2. Realistic.
3. Measurable.
4. Attainable.

The best goals will energize you and motivate you to take action! Goals will bring your life's energy into focus. Dreaming without ever focusing will dissipate your precious energy and waste your precious time. Think of goals as "dreams with deadlines," as someone once put it.

Your goals should be too exciting, too powerful, too rooted in what you already find exhilarating, for you to ignore. If the goal doesn't motivate you instantly, it needs to be revised!

Immediate Action: Take a moment to write down one important, goal in each of the following categories: financial, life style, and personal growth. A financial goal might be to earn $20,000 more per year than you're currently earning, or to get a raise by completing a key project. A lifestyle goal would relate to the way you choose to live—perhaps your goal might be to purchase a new home. And personal growth goals are those that help you answer the question, "What have I committed to do this day?" Ask yourself these questions about each goal:

- What is the person I am capable of becoming able to achieve in this area?
- In one year, in this area, what would I like to look back on and be proud of?
- To accomplish this in the next year, what would I have to do?
- Five years from now, in this area, what would I like to look back on and be proud of?
- To accomplish this in the next five years, what would I have to do?

Then, take action each week on each of these "top three goals." Keep asking yourself, "What's the next step I can take to turn this goal into a reality by the time I've set for myself?" When you figure out the answer, put the next step into your schedule...and carry it out!

Point to Ponder Before You Go On: Whatever comes to us in life, we create first in our minds. Whether we know it or not, our best dreams and goals—those that motivate us in a positive direction—are our Creator's contribution to our personal suggestion box. Judge your goals by the pictures they create in your mind and by how much they motivate you.

Chapter 24

Five Steps for Turning a Goal Into a Plan

"Noah built his ark before it started raining."
—Anonymous

The goal has been set, at least initially. What can you do to turn it into reality? Here are five simple steps you can take to expand goals—like the ones you just identified—into more detailed long-term plans.

1. Start by doing what you know works, then experiment with new applications. When in doubt, try to do more of what you're already doing that's already delivering the results you want.

2. Build the right backup scenarios into your plan. What might go wrong? Anticipate emergencies at every level of achievement, and don't let concern about your own status, as others perceive it, keep you from making the right choices in the right situations.

   There was once a young pilot who was in an emergency situation, but who wanted to appear cool to the people monitoring his flight in the tower. The pilot called in on his radio and intoned, slowly, meticulously, and calmly, "Maytag, Maytag, Maytag."

   There was a little pause while the people in the tower puzzled over this transmission.

   "Do you mean, 'Mayday, Mayday, Mayday'?" the tower finally asked.

"Yes! Yes! Mayday, for #$@#$% sake!" the pilot squeaked back in panic. He landed all right, but his desire to impress the others cost him a few seconds that could have been critical! So if you need help, ask for it quickly.

3. Get feedback from the right people on the pros and cons of your plan. People who give constructive feedback want to see you grow; people who offer only negative thoughts want to see you stay the same. Don't waste your time talking to people who want to make you feel bad about yourself.

4. Keep your eye on the goal, but don't get "target fixation." How does your goal fit into the larger pattern of your life? How does it affect your organization? What could make priorities shift? You have to keep your perspective; you have to keep your eye on the "big picture." I've heard stories of pilots who were so concentrated on their goal that they'd get hypnotized. They needed to be reminded that the point was to hit the target—but not with their airplane! That's taking target commitment a little too seriously.

5. Keep learning and growing, and remember, no one does it all alone. If the problems down the road look too large to you while you're setting up your plan, remember, you'll be a bigger person by the time you need to solve them, and you'll always have the opportunity to develop new alliances along the way. Too often, we hold off on growth because we worry, "How would I handle all those big problems I'd face?" We assume that a) We won't ever be smarter than we are right now, and b) We'll never run into anyone else who offers skills and experience that complement ours.

Once you've gotten hold of a big goal that motivates you, you need to be able to begin each and every day by breaking it down into day-to-day, hour-by-hour activities that support that goal. Break the big goal down into bite-sized portions. Ask yourself, "What one thing can I do for this hour that will help me move closer to _____?"

If you find that days are going by when you don't seem to be making even modest progress toward the goals you've identified for yourself, then it's probably time to reexamine your goals. Remember, if the goal doesn't motivate you, then there's a problem!

Having a clear-cut goal means molding that goal in clay. *Working* on that same goal on a daily basis casts it in bronze.

Immediate Action: Identify "small steps" that will point you toward "bigger steps" for each of the goals you identified in the previous chapter.

Point to Ponder Before You Go On: The formula for bitterness: Working for one thing but expecting something else!

Chapter 25

Examine
Your "Rushes"

"Your life is like a book. The title page is your name, the preface your introduction to the world. The pages are a daily record of your efforts, trials, pleasures, discouragements, and achievements. Day by day your thoughts and acts are being inscribed in your book of life. Hour by hour, the record is being made that must stand for all time. Once the word 'finis' must be written, let it then be said of your book that it is a record of noble purpose, generous service, and work well-done."
—Grenville Kleiser, author of *Training for Power and Leadership*

Lights, camera, action! Welcome to your own private Hollywood: You are making, right now, day by day, the movie of your life.

At some time in the future you will reach that great cinema in the sky. You will take a seat in that heavenly auditorium and watch the movie of your life as you lived it—playing out on the big screen to end all big screens. How will you feel about that movie as it unspools? Every night, as I go to sleep, I find myself wondering, how will "The Life and Times of Danny Cox" look when it is played back? Will I be proud of that movie? Will I know in my heart that the central character pursued the right goals, for the right reasons? Or will I wonder why on earth that man on the screen made the choices he did? Will I find myself yearning for the chance to make another film—the film I should have made? What can I do now, today, to make sure that that movie is the best I can possibly make it?

Yesterday's film is "in the can." The choices we make day by day, the goals we set for ourselves, the way we act toward achieving those goals—those are the only factors that will affect the film that still remains to be shot.

So, how can we improve that film? One way is to use the technique used by the Hollywood moguls to insure film quality: Look at the daily rushes.

What are daily rushes? They're a moviemaker's short-term answers to big questions: "Am I getting to where I thought I was getting? And if I'm not, where the heck am I getting to, and how do I get back?"

When Steven Spielberg sets out to make an exotic new adventure film, he doesn't travel around the world, shoot every scene in his script, and then sit down and review all the footage from beginning to end. That's a risky way to make a movie! Spielberg might just get to the end of the process and realize that the mood in scene 43A didn't quite match up with the mood in scene 43B—and then ask himself why he didn't notice that while he was still in Sumatra with the cast and crew.

Waiting until the last minute to review one's shooting is a dangerous proposition. Instead, a good director takes a look, each day, at the rushes, the early film clips that reflect the work that was just completed. By reviewing the first prints of that day's clips, Spielberg (and every other director worthy of the name) can evaluate each of the individual shots that will eventually turn into a movie—the movie that the director set out to make.

It's close to impossible to put together a good movie if you don't look at your rushes until the end of the production process. I believe the same principle applies to the movie of your life. And who wants to run the risk of sabotaging that release?

Rushes give filmmakers the chance to review each day's work. For a director, looking at the rushes means sitting in a dark screening room and looking out for what worked and what didn't. As he watches the images go by, the director asks questions. How should a scene be edited? What needs to be improved? How does what's up on the screen affect the next day's work?

In the same way, a barrier-breaker learns to ask questions about the "shooting schedule" of the day just past. Every day, at some point, we need to ask ourselves, "What just happened? What brought me closer to my goal? What moved me further away from my goal?

What worked? How can I get what worked to happen again—and happen on a regular basis if I need it to?"

It's just as important to ask, "What didn't work so well? What would I edit out if I had the chance? What needs to be done all over again? What do I need to do to keep a 'bad scene' from happening again?"

Even more important is to ask, "What was the big lesson life had planned for me today?" Once you figure that one out, you can ask yourself, "How well did I learn that lesson, and what can I do to put it to work the next time I face a similar situation?"

Asking questions like that, once a day, is part of reviewing the day's "rushes"—the actual events and decisions you made over the course of 24 hours. That's the way to be sure the film of your life is shaping up as it should. Watching your own daily rushes is the same as monitoring the progress you've made toward the important goals you've identified. Again, taking baby steps is fine, as long as you go somewhere you intend to go!

Immediate Action: At the end of the day today, ask yourself, "Did I move upward, toward positive role models and energizing goals, or did I move down, toward negative influences?" Be ruthlessly honest with yourself, and write down the answers you come up with on a sheet of paper. Find out whether there was a net "gain" or a net "loss" in movement toward your constructive goal, and then ask yourself how you can maximize gains and minimize losses tomorrow.

Point to Ponder Before You Go On: Examining your rushes is not an exercise in negative thinking—it's a way of fine-tuning your daily goals, and thus making progress toward your major goals. If this opportunity for self-evaluation becomes an opportunity for self-flagellation, you're in trouble! Goals always look forward; discouragement always looks backward.

Chapter 26

Seeing the Future
Almost as Clearly
as the Present

"Two years of study reveal that [hospital] patients who face difficult regimens will do far better if they sign a written contract promising to stick to the rules in return for short-term rewards.... 'We had a patient with serious kidney trouble who was very religious,' [a hospital spokesman] said. 'The nurse promised to read to her from the Bible three times a day if she limited her water intake, and it worked....' Signing a contract seems to give patients the motivation to follow the prescribed treatment....At one point in the study, patients were divided into two groups. Both groups were given intensive education about their illness and the need to follow a specific program of therapy. One group then signed written contracts; the second did not. More than 35 percent of the 'noncontract' group eventually dropped out...but no one from the group that signed contracts withdrew from their treatment."
—Orange County Register, September 22, 1976

When people can visualize rewards, they're more likely to do what's necessary to earn those rewards. What, exactly, are you working for? The vividness of your answer to that question may well determine your level of success.

No-limits achievers are always prepared to visualize the most exciting, motivating feature of their goal, and they're ready to do so in great detail. A tough old salesman I knew back when I was a salesman taught me that secret. Don't get out and hustle because you "have to," get out and meet with people because they're going to pay for your child's college education! I remember realizing after speaking with him that, if my prospects were going to be helping me send my daughters to the college they deserved to attend, I certainly had no objection to meeting with them!

Let's be honest, attaining major goals isn't always easy. If it were easy, everyone would do it! If you're selling for a living, for instance, there's a very good chance that, in order to meet that aggressive quota with the hefty bonus attached to it or win that sales contest that will entitle you to an all-expenses-paid vacation trip to Jamaica, you're going to have to encounter a few rejections along the way. If the awareness of the pain you connect with rejection is stronger than the pleasure you connect with attaining your goal, guess what's going to happen? You're going to have big problems meeting your goal!

No-limits achievers have mastered the art of making the goal they're pursuing more than vivid enough to overcome obstacles they face in the present. Take a look at the chart on the following page.

That up-and-down line on the left represents your awareness of pain as you work toward achieving a goal. The vividness of the goal runs across the bottom. The stronger the goal, the less pain you notice. Remember how boxer George Foreman dealt with physical pain in the ring? He saw what he wanted "real good," and he didn't notice the punch!

You don't have to be looking at a heavyweight challenger to put this principle to work for you. That pain in the up-and-down line might be connected to a prospect who turns you down flat, and, for good measure, tells you that your mama always dressed you funny when you were a baby and that he's got photographs to prove it. Is a conversation like that going to devastate you, or are you going to bounce right back from it?

What do you have to motivate you once that conversation is through? What's going to make you pick up the telephone and make the next call to the next prospect with just as much steam? It had better be pretty powerful. You'd better be able to picture yourself spending that bonus money on that new entertainment system you've got your eye on, or walking through the tropical sands, getting the world's best tan, or basking in the smile your daughter flashes you as she picks up her degree on graduation day.

In other words, to break through the pain barrier, the vividness of your goal has to be stronger than the pain of the obstacles you face in obtaining it. The line that runs left-to-right in the chart represents the vividness of the rewards you associate with your goals. If it's not as highly placed as the pain quotient, you won't move forward! On the other hand, your own self-discipline will automatically increase as the clarity of the goal to be achieved increases.

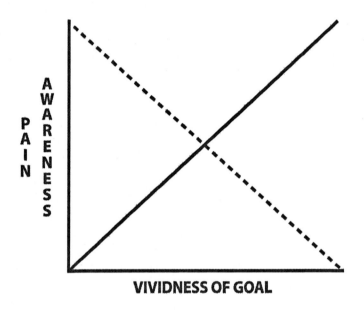

VIVIDNESS OF GOAL

Immediate Action: Take some time now to construct "mental pictures" of the pleasurable things you associate with each of your main goals. What's the most positive outcome you can associate with each goal? What do you like most about that scenario? Be as specific as you possibly can, and remember, you must be willing to be more vivid about what could go right than about what may go wrong as you pursue your goal.

Point to Ponder Before You Go On: The vividness of your goal will help you establish a high BBAQ—Bounce Back Ability Quotient!

Chapter 27

Two Goal-driven Dreamers

"To dream is to dare. To fear is to fail."
—John Goddard, explorer

A classic example of a person whose clear, compelling goals inspired her to (literally) great heights is the legendary aviatrix Jacqueline Cochran. She was the first woman to fly a bomber across the Atlantic, the first woman to fly a jet across the Atlantic, the first woman to break the sound barrier, and the first woman to make a blind landing (that is, a landing that relies completely on instruments). During her career, she held more speed, distance, and altitude records than any other pilot.

Cochran was a close friend of both Chuck Yeager and Amelia Earhart, and that's pretty good company. In 1938 she won the Bendix Trophy over a whole field of male pilots. (This was a national air race held in Cleveland, Ohio. Many of the pre-World War II air speed records were set there.) She also won the Harmon Trophy for "outstanding woman of the year" 16 times. During World War II, she was a captain in the British Air Force Auxiliary. She headed up a group of women pilots who flew military planes from manufacturing facilities to deployment sites in Europe. In 1953, Cochran set world speed records for both men and women in a Saber jet; she flew 652.552 miles an hour on a 100 kilometer course, 590.321 miles per hour on a 500 kilometer course, and 675 miles per hour on a 15-kilometer course. (That was also the year she became the first woman to break the sound barrier.) Among her many other accomplishments, she is credited with being the one who talked General Dwight D. Eisenhower into running for president!

Cochran was orphaned as a child and was raised in desperate poverty by foster parents. She started work at the tender age of eight in a cotton mill in Georgia. She became a beauty shop operator and worked in cosmetics, eventually launching her own firm. Her introduction to aviation came in part because flying was an effective—and exhilarating—way to promote her own company! In her autobiography, originally titled *Stars at Noon* in 1954 and reissued in later years as *The Autobiography of the Greatest Woman Pilot in Aviation History*, Cochran wrote, "I didn't have shoes, but I had a dream." That dream was always strong enough, and clear enough, to keep her constantly moving past the pain and obstacles she faced, and into new zones of achievement.

Another example I can offer of a setter of vivid goals—and one of the best such examples I've ever heard—is the story of the explorer John Goddard, a man I'm honored to call a close friend. At the age of 15, Goddard, a gangly teenager working on his homework, heard the voice of one of his parents' friends from the next room: "Boy, I wish I were John's age again, I'd really do things differently." Something about that remark seemed to have touched a nerve inside the boy, because he turned to a blank sheet of paper in his notebook and wrote the words, "My Life List" across the top. He began writing down goals; the first was "Explore the Nile."

The list grew to include 127 items, but that's not really what makes this story worthy of notice. What makes Goddard's story remarkable is that, over the next decades of his life, he went out and achieved the vast majority of his goals! At last count, he had experienced 108 of his original 127 adventures, both large and small. These exploits included such deeds as milking a poisonous snake (#117), flying a plane (#40), and exploring the Congo River (#3). In fact, Goddard was the first person to conduct a complete exploration of the Congo River! He also attained his goal of exploring the Nile.

John is well on his way to fulfilling another important goal from that initial list: living to see the 21st century. He keeps making new lists, and has, as of this writing, completed 415 of his goals. His most recent accomplishment: going through the Panama Canal. If there's anyone who's proved that vivid visualization of goals can lead to extraordinary levels of achievement, it's got to be John Goddard. Take a look at the list he wrote—and has constantly reviewed—and you'll get an idea of the man's talent for specifying personalized, highly motivating goals. Goddard made a point of visualizing himself accomplishing key elements of each goal, and the result was a record of exploration and discovery with few parallels in this century.

Explore:

✓1. Nile River

✓2. Amazon River

✓3. Congo River

✓4. Colorado River

5. Yangtze River, China

6. Niger River

7. Orinoco River, Venezuela

✓8. Rio Coco, Nicaragua

Study Primitive Cultures In:

✓9. The Congo

✓10. New Guinea

✓11. Brazil

✓12. Borneo

✓13. The Sudan (John was nearly buried alive in a sandstorm.)

✓14. Australia

✓15. Kenya

✓16. The Philippines

✓17. Tanganyika (now Tanzania)

✓18. Ethiopia

✓19. Nigeria

✓20. Alaska

Climb:

21. Mount Everest

22. Mount Aconcagua, Argentina

23. Mount McKinley

✓24. Mount Huascaran, Peru

✓25. Mount Kilimanjaro

✓26. Mount Ararat, Turkey

✓27. Mount Kenya

28. Mount Cook, New Zealand

✓29. Mount Popocatepetl, Mexico

✓30. The Matterhorn

✓31. Mount Rainer

✓32. Mount Fuji

✓33. Mount Vesuvius

✓34. Mount Bromo, Java

✓35. Grand Tetons

✓36. Mount Baldy, California

✓37. Carry out careers in medicine and exploration (Studied pre-med and treats illnesses among primitive tribes)

38. Visit every country in the world (30 to go)

✓39. Sudy Navaho and Hopi Indians

✓40. Learn to fly a plane

✔41. Ride horse in Rose Parade

Photograph:

✔42. Iguaco Falls, Brazil

✔43. Victoria Falls, Rhodesia (Chased by a warthog in the process)

✔44. Sutherland Falls, New Zealand

✔45. Yosemite Falls

✔46. Niagra Falls

✔47. Retrace travels of Marco Polo and Alexander the Great

Explore Underwater:

✔48. Coral reefs of Florida

✔49. Great Barrier Reef, Australia (Photographed a 300-pound clam)

✔50. Red Sea

✔51. Fiji Islands

✔52. The Bahamas

✔53. Explore Okefenokee Swamp and the Everglades

Visit:

54. North and South Poles

✔55. Great Wall of China

✔56. Panama and Suez Canals

✔57. Easter Island

✔58. The Galapagos Islands

✔59. Vatican City (Saw the Pope)

✔60. The Taj Mahal

✔61. The Eiffel Tower

✔62. The Blue Grotto

✔63. The Tower of London

✔64. The Leaning Tower of Pisa

✔65. The Sacred Well of Chichen-Itza, Mexico

✔66. Climb Ayers Rock in Australia

✔67. Follow River Jordan from Sea of Galilee to Dead Sea

Swim In:

✔68. Lake Victoria

✔69. Lake Superior

✔70. Lake Tanganyika

✔71. Lake Titicaca, South America

✔72. Lake Nicaragua

Accomplish:

✔73. Become an Eagle Scout

✔74. Dive in a submarine

✓75. Land on and take off from an aircraft carrier

✓76. Fly in a blimp, hot air ballon and glider

✓77. Ride an elephant, camel, ostrich and bronco

✓78. Skin dive to 40 feet and hold breath two and a half minutes underwater

✓79. Catch a ten-pound lobster and a ten-inch abalone

✓80. Play flute and violin

✓81. Type 50 words a minute

✓82. Take a parachute jump

✓83. Learn water and snow skiing

✓84. Go on a church mission

✓85. Follow the John Muir Trail

✓86. Study native medicines and bring back useful ones

✓87. Bag camera trophies of elephant, lion, rhino, cheetah, cape buffalo and whale

✓88. Learn to fence

✓89. Learn jujitsu

✓90. Teach a college course

✓91. Watch a cremation ceremony in Bali

✓92. Explore depths of the sea

93. Appear in a Tarzan movie (He now considers this an irrelevant boyhood dream)

94. Own a horse, chimpanzee, cheetah, ocelot and coyote (Yet to own a chimp or cheetah)

95. Become a ham radio operator

✓96. Build own telescope

✓97. Write a book (On Nile trip)

✓98. Publish an article in *National Geographic* Magazine

✓99. High jump five feet

✓100. Broad jump 15 feet

✓101. Run a mile in five minutes

✓102. Weigh 175 pounds stripped (still does)

✓103. Perform 200 sit-ups and 20 pull-ups

✓104. Learn French, Spanish and Arabic

105. Study dragon lizards

on Komodo Island (Boat broke down within 20 miles of island)

✓106. Visit birthplace of Grandfather Sorenson in Denmark

✓107. Visit birthplace of Grandfather Goddard in England

✓108. Ship aboard a freighter as a seaman

109. Read the entire *Encyclopedia Britannica* (Has read extensive parts in each volume)

✓110. Read the Bible from cover to cover

✓111. Read the works of Shakespeare, Plato, Aristotle, Dickens, Thoreau, Poe, Rousseau, Bacon, Hemingway, Twain, Burroughs, Conrad, Talmage, Tolstoi, Longfellow, Keats, Whittier and Emerson (Not every work of each)

✓112. Become familiar with the compositions of Bach, Beethoben, Debussy, Ibert, Mendelssohn, Lalo, Rimski-Korsakov, Respighi, Liszt, Rachmaninoff, Stravinsky, Toch, Tschaikovsky, Verdi

✓113. Become proficient in the use of a plane, motorcycle, tractor, surfboard, rifle, pistol, canoe, microscope, football, bow and arrow, lariat and boomerang

✓114. Compose music

✓115. Play *Clair de Lune* on the piano

✓116. Watch fire-walking ceremony (In Bali and Surinam)

✓117. Milk a poisonous snake (Bitten by a diamond back during a photo session)

✓118. Light a match with a 22 rifle

✓119. Visit a movie studio

✓120. Climb Cheops' pyramid

✓121. Become a member of the Explorers' Club and Adventurers' Club

✓122. Learn to play polo

✓123. Travel through the Grand Canyon on foot and by boat

✓124. Circumnavigate the globe (four times)

125. Visit the moon ("Someday if God wills")

✓126. Marry and have children (Has five children)

✓127. Live to see the 21st Century

(Reproduced by permission of John Goddard.)

Immediate Action: Reevaluate the goals you've set for yourself once again. Keep focusing on them until they are as motivating as the ones that drove Cochran and Goddard to no-limits performance time and time again.

Point to Ponder Before You Go On: Rely on it: Your daily progress can never exceed your daily goals.

Chapter 28

Building Tomorrows vs. Repeating Yesterdays

"It's no good running a pig farm badly for 30 years while saying, 'Really, I was meant to be a ballet dancer.' By that time, pigs will be your style."
—Quentin Crisp, author of *Doing It With Style*

L ots of people struggle for a definition of true fulfillment. Not the barrier-breakers I've worked with. To them, fulfillment has a calling card: an unmistakable, gut-level feeling that they're "on the right track."

Often, when you are on the right track you will have a strong sense of purpose. By this I mean that you'll have a powerful sense that what you are doing is the right thing for you to be doing. You'll have a deep faith that where you are going is the right place for you to be going. You may find that you don't even have to think too much about whether or not you've embarked on the right course of action; what you've committed to feels nearly perfect. The people you're meeting, the tools you're acquiring, the places you're visiting, are all the right ones. You are moving in a positive direction. You get a sense that something new and significant has happened, each and every day.

How can you tell whether you're on the right track? Simple. Stop and ask yourself whether you're having fun on a regular basis, more so than ever before. How's that for a straightforward self-diagnostic test? The whole experience of expanding one's horizons, developing one's capabilities, moving beyond the comfort zone—all of which adds up to what I call in my speeches "building a tomorrow"—is *enjoyable*.

Don't misunderstand; the process can be intense, and it can be demanding. But at the end of the day, it's also fun—much more fun than repeating a predetermined set of patterns for their own sake. I think God meant the process of building a tomorrow to be enjoyable. He hoped we'd get addicted to it. I think He also took pains to make the process of dwelling on the same dreary problems and perceived impossibilities as exhausting, frustrating, and monotonous as it could possibly be. He *didn't* want us to get hooked on that syndrome. And yet somehow we manage to find ways to become accustomed to the process of *not* working toward our constructive goals.

Goals are all upstream. Moving toward them yields tremendous satisfaction, but moving toward them also takes work. Your life's purpose, your "destiny goals," must be more inspiring and powerful than that accumulation of negative, uninspiring habits that constantly threaten to draw you back into a "safe" routine, a problem you wrestle with but never quite pin down and defeat. I call these self-defeating assumptions, which hold back no-limits performance, *self-imposed barriers*. They're the primary obstacle to building new tomorrows and the main justification for repeating yesterday. Remember Charlie, the salesperson who found a way to earn $2,000 a month, no matter what? Before he got motivated to push past that level, he was a perfect example of someone who was struggling with a self-imposed barrier.

Why aren't we better at stepping forward and solving these problems, problems that have been around for so long in our lives? Well, we'd have to get ready to face the new problems of the future if we did that. At least the problems we never quite solve are familiar to us. All too often, we sabotage our own efforts to reach our goals by paying homage to self-imposed barriers that frighten us *less* than what might happen in the future (including our own success). The tragic myth sounds like this: "If I can keep on repeating yesterday, I won't have to face the demands of tomorrow." It's a lie!

Self-imposed barriers...are often accompanied by words such as, "We've always done it that way" or, "I did the best I could under the circumstances." These common justifications leave out the possibility that there could be *other* ways to address an issue, or that we have the power to change our circumstances. Traditionally accepted self-imposed barriers are a primary reason for the organizational productivity meltdown known as "nostalgic paralysis." As conductor and opera director Kurt Herbert Adler put it, "Tradition is what you resort to when you don't have the time or money to do it right."

*Self-imposed barriers...*are self-constructed handicaps, rooted in fear of the future, that block what would otherwise be a clear road. What causes these handicaps? "Ghosts that ain't," as we said back home.

*Self-imposed barriers...*are habitual stumbling blocks that show up again and again. They're problems that we've learned not to address over the years. "My time-planning skills are never going to be as good as so-and-so's." "I'm not good with computer software and I never have been. I probably never will be." Remember, the person whose skills you are admiring was probably once less proficient than you are right now.

*Self-imposed barriers...*are entrenched habits that keep you from learning new things. If it's "not your job" to learn how customers actually use your product or service, you may never find out what's keeping that product from taking off in the marketplace.

*Self-imposed barriers...*are examples of *not* doing what we know works. If you know full well that your boss reacts badly to a certain way of presenting technical information, and you know he reacts well to another method of presenting the same data, there's no excuse for not following the path that you know will result in a full, open-minded assessment of what you've discovered.

*Self-imposed barriers...*are situations where we talk ourselves into giving less than our level best. We *always* have a choice: to give our level best or not to. Choosing to give our level best means being open to new ideas—and building a tomorrow. Choosing *not* to give our level best means closing down to new ideas—and repeating yesterday. If you don't try something new, guess what happens? Nothing changes!

*Self-imposed barriers...*are at the upper limit of your comfort zone. They're the borders that separate no-limits performance from mediocre performance. If you're not tackling one of your own self-imposed barriers, odds are you're not moving forward.

*Removing self-imposed barriers by giving our level best every time means...*improving our own morale and the morale of others, deepening feelings of wholeness and integrity in all aspects of our lives, and increasing our sense of "being on the right track."

Self-imposed barriers are lethal. They kill personal fulfillment and feelings of accomplishment and satisfaction. What's more, if we don't recognize them and take action to turn them around, they get stronger over time. Repeating yesterday over and over again makes us blind to our remaining potential. In other words: A bad habit can become so strong that it can actually be mistaken for destiny. Once you believe a self-imposed barrier is your destiny, you're not fully alive. Once you reject the possibility of change, you say no to tomorrow...and yes to yesterday.

Reversing self-imposed barriers is far easier than most of us imagine. Self-imposed barriers have a way of evaporating when discomfort with the current situation finally turns to enough pain to make us change the way we do things. If Bob's boss were to tell him he'd be fired if he didn't stop showing up for work late, I'm betting Bob would find a way to show up for work on time. This raises some important questions: Why should Bob wait for a lecture from his boss? Why should Bob grant his boss the authority to change his behavior, when it's Bob who ultimately changes his own behavior anyway? Why shouldn't Bob ask himself, "If I'm holding something back, why am I doing that? And if I hold nothing back, what could be accomplished?"

We're tied with straws...and we think they're chains.

So are you building a tomorrow or are you repeating a yesterday? My experience is that, if you truly have a sense that you are moving in the right direction, that you're expanding your skills and applying them to new situations, you'll know it. And if your work is feeding into old habits, old assumptions, old limitations, you'll know that, too, because that process is downright exhausting and likely to leave you feeling that all you've accomplished at the end of the day is to wear a little more off your own tread.

When you have a "right direction" moment, it is not only exciting, but your awareness increases. "Wow, this can be really exciting when I pull this off." "This can lead to great things." No more repeated yesterdays!

Remember: Out of goal orientation comes self-discipline. Out of self-discipline comes high achievement. Out of high achievement comes personal freedom—but not the kind of "personal freedom" we associate with excess or a failure to assume personal responsibility. The kind of freedom I'm talking about is rooted in a strong personal character, a sense of being "in tune" with God's plan for you.

Repeating yesterday...puts a lid on undeveloped potential and freezes you at your current level of competence. (In fact, a small success can often paralyze a person into a long string of repeated yesterdays.)

Repeating yesterday...centers on reaction to familiar problems, not action to achieve new goals.

Repeating yesterday...means giving away the ability to believe, deep in your heart, that your best is yet to come.

Repeating yesterday...means surrendering leadership of your life in exchange for the right to complete familiar day-to-day tasks.

Repeating yesterday...is false security.

Repeating yesterday...is hypnotic.

Repeating yesterday...is habit-driven.

Repeating yesterday...means you're always losing ground.

Immediate Action: Think of the most productive, happiest people you've worked with over the years—people who refused to fall into the trap of believing that, by repeating yesterday, they could avoid the challenges of tomorrow. Can you think of a self-imposed barrier that would have severely limited one of these people? What did that person do to turn that limiting habit or assumption around?

Point to Ponder Before You Go On: The more excited you become about your positive goals, the more likely you are to get your own self-imposed barriers to fall—and the more likely you are to stop spending your precious time and energy repeating yesterdays.

Chapter 29

Making Habits
Work for You,
for a Change

*"The tragedy of life is not that it ends so soon, but that we
wait so long to begin it."*
—Richard L. Evans, author

Repeating yesterday, as you just saw, is a habit-driven process. Fortunately, not every habit is connected to the trap of reinforcing self-imposed barriers. Some are very healthy. Consider the habit of showing up for work on time or brushing your teeth on a regular basis.

Constructive habits can take the form of personal success rituals—actions you perform almost automatically and that help you boost your Bounce Back Ability Quotient. No-limits achievers know they need a ritual that is (at least) as powerful as their disappointments, something that helps them place things in perspective when they experience a challenge or lose a little altitude on the way to achieving a goal. That's the kind of habit you want to develop and reinforce.

It's easy to lose perspective when you've been working toward a goal for a while. Setbacks can seem like disasters, because you've been working so hard and because you're so close to the action. Habit can be a tool to help you overcome those feelings of discomfort and depression that can set in when things seem larger than they really are.

As a rule, habit loves the status quo. Yet, when habit is turned into a method of progress on a continuing basis, habit can be put to very good use. As the foundation of a personal success ritual—for instance, a willingness to ask yourself, "What did I learn from this situation, and how can I apply it to the next challenge I face?"—habit can result in a new and stronger commitment to your goal and essential "backup plans" that will benefit you down the line.

If your habit helps you to grow more, to break from the status quo, to make that right-hand turn out of the familiar and into the zone of high achievement, then habit can be beneficial. It can help you exceed your "personal best" again and again. And while physical record-breaking can usually go on only for so long, the habitual development of new mental areas can help you continue to break barriers for a lifetime.

My friend Jim Raco liked to say, "You never work hard to pay bills. You work hard to have fun with the money. Otherwise, you won't have enough to do either one of them—pay bills or have fun!" As you can see from that comment, he knew how to focus on the most exciting aspects of his goals. And yet, like many other salespeople, he sometimes felt down when a sale that he'd put his heart and soul into went sour. How did he get himself back up? I asked him that once. The answer was simple: He had a habit for success.

Jim said, "Whenever a sale goes down in flames, I drive up to Mulholland Drive in the Santa Monica mountains. There's one point where you can see the entire San Fernando Valley. Up to that point, of course, I've usually been finding lots of little ways to tell myself that the real estate sale I just lost was the last house in the valley, that I had just blown that opportunity, and that my business is now over. Then I look at all those houses out there in the valley and I think 'How am I going to get to 'em all?' And I come down off that mountain motivated. I can hardly wait to get to the next house I'm supposed to sell!"

Immediate Action: What's your ritual for success? Develop a routine that can help you generate a habitual positive response when obstacles appear. (They will!)

Point to Ponder Before You Go On: Either you harness habit or habit harnesses you.

Chapter 30

Every Barrier
Can Be Overcome!

"Dear Lord, remind me that the sins I've committed and the wrongs I have not righted today need not haunt me tomorrow, but can be forgiven; and, at the same time, help me to remember that the most I have accomplished today is not good enough for tomorrow."
—Tom Haggai, author of *How the Best Is Won*

If you're looking for evidence that human beings can find a way to make it over any and every obstacle and self-imposed barrier, look no further. There's a lady I'd like you to meet.

At the company where I worked, we had a real estate agent named Mary Lawrence. Before she hooked up with us, she'd had an automobile accident and had suffered brain damage and some permanent memory loss. So she got a tiny handheld tape recorder, and when she was talking with buyers she would record the conversation. On the phone, she would record her half of the conversation, being careful to reiterate all the important details the client was providing. Then, at home, she would make notes from the tapes. Using this system, she was able to become an outstanding agent.

Mary had been impressive from the beginning; I'll never forget how she landed her job with us. She called me up one day and said, in a very firm and assured tone of voice, "I want to talk to you about going to work for you." Talk about taking the direct approach! I liked the way she talked, and when she came in to interview, I liked her directness and the way she focused so clearly on what we were doing. I didn't realize it was part of her way of dealing with the results of her permanent brain damage.

We had an outstanding training program and she sailed right through it and went on to become the outstanding rookie salesperson of the year. We held our awards banquet at the Disneyland Hotel. I presented her with the trophy that signified that she was one of our top-10 first-year salespeople. There I was in my tux; there she was in her fancy dress. She looked at the award for a long moment and then said, "Hold my place, because I'll be back up here next year." She wasn't satisfied with being one of the best *rookie* salespeople—she wanted to win the award for top salesperson in the organization, period.

The very next day, she went out and bought a long pink dress to wear for the presentation the next year! She hung it right in the middle of her closet. That dress reminded her each day that she had things to do that day to achieve her goal. By awards time the next year, she was the top salesperson in our organization. When she walked across the floor in that long pink dress to receive her award, the band was playing "The Impossible Dream" and the entire company rose to its feet in applause. Many of us had tears in our eyes. I know I did.

Immediate Action: Our star salesperson had blasted right through the four common roadblocks to overcoming barriers. Think of ways you can follow her example in your own life in each of the four areas.

1. Prejudgment. She didn't say to herself, "That goal-orientation stuff might work for other people, but it wouldn't work for me."
2. Lack of resources. She didn't say to herself, "I don't have the time (or money or energy) to do that."
3. Comfort of old habits. She didn't fall into the trap of relying on old patterns of behavior that had "always worked before."
4. Reliance on external motivation. She didn't wait for the support of a boss, or her colleagues, or her friends before she set her sights on what she wanted.

Point to Ponder Before You Go On: We've all known people who talked on and on about their bad luck. That's one way to pass the time, but in the end, spending all your time thinking about what *doesn't* work means you get about as much out of life as a hearse!

Chapter 31

The Guy on the White Horse

"Rise early. Work hard. Strike oil."
–J. Paul Getty's formula for success

Sometimes, people set up goals for themselves and then find reasons to keep themselves from making any meaningful progress toward those goals. Perhaps you've run into people who have established "deserve levels" for themselves—levels of income, or happiness, or career satisfaction that they never go much above or much below, despite the opportunity to do so.

Think about financial goals. Even people who have work situations that allow for wide disparities in monthly income totals—salespeople, say, or home entrepreneurs—somehow manage to keep themselves from moving much outside of this so-called "comfort level." Although people will say that they want to be able to increase their incomes, they'll often find some way to link the attainment of that goal to someone other than themselves, and their small steps won't match up with the big goals they've set up. The distance between where they are and where they want to be is measured in excuses: "If only someone would take over the job of organizing things..." "If only our financial system were better targeted..." "If only I had the energy I once had..."

There are far too many unfortunate souls on this earth who think that, once they figure out what life's all about, they'll be able to press the "rewind" button and run themselves back to, say, age 21—or any other time when "things were better." Sad to say, people don't come equipped with such a button. For these poor folks, life slips by, day by day, as they wait for someone or something to show them the way.

What they're waiting for, when you get right down to it, is the "guy on the white horse"—the person who will tackle all the mysteries, solve all the problems, ride in and rescue them. While they're

117

waiting for this person to show up, they disengage. Let me share a secret: You have instant access to the "man or woman on the white horse"—the person on whom our safety and success depends—at any time. All you have to do is look down, and you'll see that you're sitting astride that "white horse."

You are the guy on the white horse! You are the only person who's qualified to change your present and, thereby, change your future. Don't wait for great occasions to step forward as your own hero; don't assume that someone else is blocking your way. Seize common occasions for positive personal change, and *make* them great.

The time to commit yourself to developing the most efficient plan possible to achieve your goals is right now. And the person who must carry out that plan is you. As someone once said, "If it is to be, it is up to me."

Immediate Action: Think about how can you take action, today, to address a challenge you had once believed to be someone else's responsibility. Waiting for someone else to achieve a goal for us means abandoning that "molded-in-clay" goal—before it's been put into permanent form!

Point to Ponder Before You Go On: Remember: A bad habit—like waiting for the guy on the white horse—can become so strong that it can be mistaken for destiny. Don't let that happen to you!

Chapter 32

Wildebeest
Thinking

*"What do you have planned for the next six months? How do
you think you did over the last six months? What are you
doing right now?"*
—Walt Disney's three questions to those who reported to him

To reach your goals, you have to avoid what I call "wildebeest
thinking." Some time ago, I had the pleasure of taking an
early-morning hot-air balloon flight over the Serengetti Plain
with the remarkable John Goddard. (See Chapter 27.) The scene was
beautiful; you could see the elephants, the lions, and the great waves
of wildebeest storming across the plain. "It's a good thing there are
so many of them," mused our African guide, who had noticed me
staring at the huge gatherings of wildebeest. "Otherwise, that species
would die out in a hurry."

I asked him what he meant. He smiled and pointed to a wildebeest that had stopped in its tracks. "You'll notice that the wildebeest
never run for very long. That's not because they've just realized
something important and want to stop and think about it. And it's not
because they're tired. It's because they're so dumb that they forget
why they started running in the first place. They see a predator, they
realize they're supposed to run away, and they start moving in the
opposite direction. But they lose sight of what inspired them to run,
sometimes at the most inopportune moments. I've seen them stop
running right next to a predator; sometimes they'll walk right up to
one, as though they weren't really sure whether this is the same ani-
mal that frightened them a few minutes ago. They almost seem to be
saying, 'Hey, Mr. Lion, are you hungry? Care for some lunch?' If
there weren't a whole lot of wildebeest, I think the whole species
would get gobbled up in a matter of weeks."

It was easy to laugh at the wildebeest while I was on the balloon, but before that flight was over, I found myself with the funny feeling that I'd seen that same kind of problem in the business world.

Aren't there are a lot of people whose regular behavior reminds you of the wildebeest? They get a great idea, they commit themselves to a goal, and they run with that goal for a day or maybe for only a half a day. Maybe they just walk around, gingerly, for 15 minutes or so. After that 15 minutes of ambling around, they realize they haven't gotten to where they said they wanted to get to. Then they say to themselves, "Hmm, this is going to be tough; it isn't as easy as I thought it was going to be." And they stop dead in their tracks.

These people are the victims of habitual wildebeest thinking. Often, their problem isn't that they're doing the wrong things to move closer to their goals—they're not doing anything to move closer to their goals.

To avoid wildebeest thinking, you have to set a goal and then stick to it. You don't want to stop in your tracks, and you certainly don't want to stop when your predators are close by. You have to take stock at the end of each and every day and ask yourself, "How much closer am I to the major goals I set for myself?" And if the honest answer to that question is that you haven't made any meaningful movement toward the goals you've identified—if you've stopped in your tracks—then you have to resolve to do something different the next time you find yourself on the plains of the Serengetti! No one wants to be lion lunch.

I'd venture to guess that wildebeest never, ever have a clear sense of the overall direction of their day. They don't know whether or not they're moving closer to or further away from a goal, and they certainly don't seem to be very good at embracing goals that inspire them (or anyone else). Wildebeest don't build tomorrows. They live in a "permanent yesterday," a world ruled by unproductive habit, inertia, and routine. You've already read about the dangers of this "yesterday" mentality. The routine may be comforting, but it can also be lethal—as heaven knows how many wildebeest have discovered firsthand and a little too late for their own good.

Those routines only *seem* comfortable and safe to us. They're not *really* comfortable—they just seem less scary, for the moment, than the last thing we remembered to challenge ourselves with. If we thought things through, we'd realize that it was the deadening routines we allow into our lives that are truly scary. Think about it. Some routines—like, say, forgetting why you were running away from a lion just a minute ago—might just lead you to find yourself turning into someone else's appetizer. That's about as far away from comfort as anyone is likely to get.

Most of us encounter wildebeest thinking from time to time in our own lives. (I know I do.) The trick is not to let that kind of thinking take over the day. At the close of the day, you have to be able to ask yourself, "Was I pursuing positive goals, goals based on my image of the best person I'm capable of being, or was I drifting downward toward negative influences that are likely to stop my progress toward positive goals?" If, as you look back over your day's journey, you realize that you made a habit of stopping because you forgot why you started running in the first place, beware! A wildebeest may be taking over your day.

Recognizing that you're indulging in wildebeest thinking means you've gotten a big part of the job done. Once you recognize that you've stalled out, you can start moving away from that lion. The aim is to be able to say, at the end of the day, "You know what? I tried some new things today; getting to my goal is harder than I thought it would be, and it might take me longer to get where I'm going than I thought it would, but I tried something. And I'm going to try something else tomorrow." That's the way to get the jump on the predators.

Don't make the mistake of assuming that the predator is (necessarily) a competitor or a rival. It could be you! For instance, if you stop moving toward constructive goals long enough to start thinking about compromising your own ethical principles, you're in trouble. That's a wildebeest standing right next to a lion, saying, "Care for an hors d'oeuvre?" It's time to start thinking about new approaches— strategies that will allow you to maintain your own ethical standards *and* shoot for the goals that get you jazzed up.

Immediate Action: Think of a person you know who engaged in "wildebeest thinking"—someone who was easily distracted and stopped paying attention to key objectives at any and every opportunity. What setbacks did this person have to face as a result? (As a rule, wildebeest thinkers only serve as examples of what *not* to do.)

Point to Ponder Before You Go On: The wildebeest never tries anything new—no matter what happens! Barrier-breakers know better. Once they've tried something, once they're no longer standing still, they're no longer subject to the wildebeest mind-set. They're on the move.

Chapter 33

Talk to Strengths, Be Aware of Weaknesses

"Good judgment comes from experience. And where does experience come from? Experience comes from bad judgment."
—Mark Twain

Many people make the mistake of focusing constantly on their weaknesses, and only allowing themselves a minimal awareness of their strong suits. It's the person we are capable of becoming—not the person who has held us back in the past—who must be the focus of our attention. When we first focus with attention and intensity on what we're doing that's working, and then become aware of the areas where we need to grow, we strengthen our sense of purpose. Self-confidence grows. Negative self-talk is far less likely to be a problem.

So, what are you already doing right?

Ted Williams used to take batting practice while delivering a loud, running monologue about the beauty of the towering drives he was launching. (Truth be told, they were pretty impressive.) Talking to your strengths, as Williams did, helps build up self-esteem and increases the likelihood that your next swing of the bat will result in a home run.

Does that mean you never make mistakes? Of course not. High achievers are constantly on the lookout for situations where they've made unproductive commitments to the status quo, often without even realizing it. They're aware of their weaknesses. They know it's their own fault if they get stuck making the same mistake over and over again, but they also know that they always have the opportunity to take the new road—to take that hard right turn into new achievement. The trouble is that they may continue to fail to see a problem area, so they're always on the lookout for new ways to improve themselves. But they don't fixate on weaknesses. They fixate on strengths.

Show me not your strengths, but your own estimate of your strengths, and I will predict your future!

Immediate Action: Make a list of 10 skills you already possess and have already developed highly enough to allow you to make a significant contribution to your organization, and to your future.

Point to Ponder Before You Go On: Focusing on your strengths gets you eager to speak the five most exciting words in the English language: "It's time to get started!"

Chapter 34

Dead Fish,
Live Fish

"No matter how strongly and perfectly constructed, or how powerful a locomotive may be, unless the water is heated to 212 degrees, the train will not move an inch. Warm water, water even at the boiling point, will not answer."
—Elbert Hubbard

It's time to ask yourself, "How strong is my sense of purpose?" Is it strong enough to propel you out of the cycle of habits that aren't moving you toward your goal?

Only your own force of will, your own mental attitude, can establish a force strong enough to ensure that you can break through an unproductive habit. When you embrace change, you have to embrace it with every cell of your being, otherwise yesterday's way of doing things has a way of creeping in and claiming your attention.

A century ago, Elbert Hubbard made a timeless observation: "Even a dead fish can go downstream; it takes a live one to go against the current." The currents of habit are strong—very strong! The price you will have to pay to manage that "right-hand turn" out of deadening routine and into a new, more productive, more stimulating way of living is to *control your own mental attitude*. That means consciously guiding your emotions and putting an end to thoughtless, habitual responses.

There Are No Limits

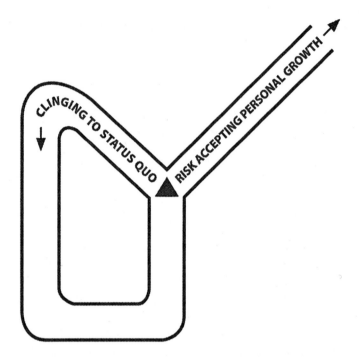

CLINGING TO STATUS QUO

1. No Goals
2. Stagnation
3. Boredom
4. Amusement
5. Existence
6. Deterioration
7. Problems
8. Victim Of Situation
9. Making A Living
10. Having Something To Live On

(Describe One Year From Today
On This Road)

RISK ACCEPTING PERSONAL GROWTH

1. New Goals
2. Progress
3. Adventure
4. Enjoyment
5. Vitality
6. Development
7. Problems
8. Master Of Situation
9. Making A Life
10. Having Something To Live For

(Describe One Year From Today
On This Road)

Ambition and self-discipline increase at the same rate; in fact, they reinforce each other. Your mental attitude will determine the strength of the "countercurrent" you generate in trying to overcome an old, unproductive habit, such as procrastination, a perpetually cluttered desk, a tendency to blame others, or an addiction to worst-case-scenario thinking.

If you're like most people, you'll find that the current you're swimming against is stronger during some parts of the day than it is during others. Learn to make the most of your "prime time!" When does the sun rise inside you, and at what time does it set? In other words, what's the best time of day for you to take on the job of eradicating a habit that isn't helping you? For some of us, early in the morning is the very best time of day to try to install a new way of doing things, such as organizing a new filing system or beginning a new cold-calling routine.

Here's another technique you can use to move yourself into the "live fish" category: When you come across a good idea, take action on it immediately, or at least as close to immediately as you can manage. Suppose you've just taken part in a management-training seminar, and you've found out about some excellent strategies for improving your communication with your team members. *Isolate the three best ideas and implement them within 72 hours!* My experience—both as a manager and as someone who's helped to boost the productivity of others through seminars and taped programs—is that any good idea left "on the shelf" for more than three days has a funny way of staying on that shelf indefinitely. When you learn something new, if you haven't used it within 72 hours, that learning experience was a waste of time, money, and energy!

Another great strategy for improving your mental attitude and strengthening your sense of purpose: Take full advantage of this book. At the beginning and end of each chapter and at the conclusion of each main section, you'll find some of the most inspiring words I've ever come across on transcending perceived limits, developing a sense of purpose, fostering a spirit of adventure, and committing to ongoing growth. Take advantage of these opportunities to expand your horizons.

Finally—and this is vitally important—don't underestimate the importance of committing your goals to writing and reviewing them regularly. Remember, goals are meant to motivate you! The act of writing down a goal—maybe in the present tense, as in "I am closing $X in sales this quarter"—is a powerful mental stimulant. So is using a pen and notepad to break goals down into daily, bite-sized portions.

I believe strongly in committing big goals to writing, because I've seen first-hand—both in my own life and the lives of others—how powerful and effective the act of setting goals down on paper can be.

John Goddard's remarkable list—and his endless dedication to checking items off of it—didn't happen as the result of an accident. In order to emerge as one of the modern world's premier explorers, Goddard has become a master of the art of visualization. He's used the act of writing—and ceaselessly reviewing—his goals as a spur to seeing himself completing each of the tasks he'd assigned himself. It worked, and you can make it work in your life, too. So take this opportunity to review the written goals you established for yourself in Chapter 23. Which have the strongest emotional effect on you? Revise them—on paper—until they carry enough "why" power to carry you upstream. The goals you write out must help you meet Edison's definition of the successful person—one who has "the ability to apply...physical and mental energies to one problem incessantly without growing weary."

Immediate Action: Take a look at the "crossroads" graphic on page 126. Describe, in detail and in writing, what your life will be like one year from today if you habitually follow the path of least resistance—that easy left-hand turn. Then describe what your life will be like one year from today if you build up the habit of making the right turn toward risk-accepting personal growth.

Point to Ponder Before You Go On: If your enthusiastic mental attitude dies on you, the most likely reason is simple: You forgot to feed it! Fortunately, you can revive it—and strengthen your own sense of purpose—by using the ideas that appear in this section of the book. (See the next chapter for even more insights and ideas.)

Chapter 35

Guiding Voices:
Your Driving Purpose

Here are insights on the subject of purpose from some of the world's
Master Teachers.

"There is no failure except in no longer trying. There is no defeat
except from within, no really insurmountable barrier save our own
inherent weakness of purpose."
—Elbert Hubbard

"Wouldn't it be Hell if God showed you what you could have
been—and what you could have done?"
—Fred Smith, author of *You and Your Network*

"Come to the edge!
(It's too high!)
Come to the edge!
(We might fall!)
Come to the edge!
And he pushed them...and they flew!"
—Christopher Logue, poet

"You cannot wait for inspiration; you must go after it with a
club."
—Anonymous

"Purpose channels everything else....Without the sense of purpose, the spirit of adventure can go in many different directions,
and the capacity for growth probably would not be realized as completely."
—Jim Newton

"No individual has any right to come into the world and go out of it without leaving distinct and legitimate reasons for having passed through it."
—George Washington Carver

"There is no tonic, no stimulant like that of the successful pursuit of one's highest ambition."
—Orison Swett Marden

"Some people bear three kinds of trouble—all they ever had, all they have now, and all they expect to have."
—Edward Everett Hale

"Nothing can work me damage except myself; the harm that I sustain, I carry about with me, and never am a real sufferer but by my own fault."
—St. Bernard

"Money wasn't that important (to me). Money doesn't help you sleep....Money doesn't make your brother stay interested in his studies. Money doesn't help an argument when nobody knows what they're arguing about."
—George Foreman

"Happiness comes to those who are moving toward something they want very much to happen. And it almost always involves making someone else happy."
—Earl Nightingale, broadcaster and author

"A man's life is what his thoughts make of it."
—Marcus Aurelius

"A man of stature has no need of status."
—Charles Hendrickson Brower, chairman of the board of Batten, Barton, Durstine, and Osborne

"It is said that Bunyan, during the years he was in jail, became so absorbed in some of the characters in Pilgrim's Progress, and was so carried away with them, that he would often fall upon his knees and shed tears of joy in his ecstasies. His imagination transformed his prison into a Palace Beautiful. The jail walls did not confine his mind or his imagination. He lived in the town of Vanity Fair; he climbed the delectable mountain. Stone walls do not a prison make for such a spirit of happiness as Bunyan possessed. Think of this wonderful man imprisoned for 12 years, and yet, in spite of all he suffered, producing a book only second to the Bible!"
—Orison Swett Marden, *The Joys Of Living*

"I am as bad as the worst, but thank God, I am as good as the best."
—Walt Whitman

"The real voyage of discovery consists not in seeking new landscapes, but in having new eyes."
—Marcel Proust

"The great and glorious masterpiece of man is to know how to live with a purpose."
—Montaigne

"I would rather be ashes than dust! I would rather that my spark should burn out in a brilliant blaze, than it should be stifled by dry rot. I would rather be a superb meteor, every atom of me in magnificent glow, than a sleepy and permanent planet. The proper function of man is to live, not to exist. I shall not waste my days in trying to prolong them. I shall use my time."
—Jack London

"Anyone who limits her vision to memories of yesterday is already dead."
—Lillie Langtry, English actress

"When a thing is done, it's done. Don't look back. Look forward to your next objective."
—General George C. Marshall

131

"I've found that when you make a deep commitment, unseen forces come to your aid."
—Charles Lindbergh

"No sculptor can call out of the marble a grander model than the one in his mind."
—Orison Swett Marden

"Man is an infinite little copy of God—that is glory enough for man....Little as I am, I feel the God in me."
—Victor Hugo

"A fault acknowledged is half-cured."
—Anonymous

"Fences were built for those who cannot fly."
—Elbert Hubbard

"Happiness is incompatible with stagnation."
—Orison Swett Marden

"No crime is so great to the envious as that of daring to excel."
—Pliny the Younger

"Loyalty to petrified opinion never yet broke a chain or freed a human soul."
—Mark Twain

"I am in the place where I ought to be."
—Isaak Dinesen, author of *Out of Africa*

"The moment you resolve to take hold of life with all your might and make the most of yourself at any cost, to sacrifice all lesser ambitions to your one great aim, to cut loose from everything that interferes with this aim, to stand alone, firm in your purpose, whatever happens, you set in motion the divine inner forces the Creator has implanted in you for your own development. Live up to your resolve, work as the Creator meant you to work for the perfecting of His plan,

and you will be invincible. No power on earth can hold you back from success."
—Orison Swett Marden

"I looked around for a helping hand—found it! At the end of my arm! And there was another one just like it at the end of the other arm."
—Jim Rohn, speaker and author

"Destiny is not a matter of chance, it is a matter of choice; it is not a thing to be waited for, it is a thing to be achieved."
—William Jennings Bryan

"Executives, athletes, and other professionals regularly use guided imagery or visualization to promote learning and open paths to achievement. How it works: Relax, close your eyes, and visualize yourself achieving a specific success, such as landing a new account or solving a complex problem. Then ask yourself what must happen for the image to become reality. Why it works: Images provide us with insights we can't always put into words."
—Excerpted in *Boardroom Reports,* from *The Learning Edge: How Smart Managers Stay That Way,* by Calhoun W. Wick

Part 3:

Your Spirit
Of Adventure

Chapter 36

Fear vs. Courage:
It's Your Choice

"Once when Marshall Ney was going into battle, looking down at his knees which were smiting together, he said, 'You may well shake; you would shake worse yet if you knew where I am going to take you.' Napoleon was so much impressed with the courage and resources of Marshal Ney, that he said, 'I have two hundred millions in my coffers, and I would give them all for Ney.'"
—Orison Swett Marden

What or who builds self-imposed barriers? A stonemason named Fear, one who is highly skilled in building powerful barriers from nonexistent stones. Where does this craftsman live? In our minds. He's always there, but it's up to us whether he lives in the back of our minds or the front of our minds.

Fear is the sworn enemy of adventure, which is the third and perhaps most exhilarating force driving no-limits achievement. And Fear goes exactly where we tell him to go.

We move Fear from the back of our minds to the front of our minds by shifting our concentration away from our own courage, and choosing instead to focus on that which frightens us. Not only does that action change Fear's location, but through the process of concentration, it means we actually start to strengthen Fear. Fear has no strength of its own; its only strength is that which we *choose* to give it.

When Fear defeats us, it does so because of our own mental focus. And unfortunately, the strength we pass along to Fear is the very strength we need to overcome it! If, on the other hand, we choose to push our goals, wrapped in courage, to the forefront of our minds, then barriers break.

You already possess sufficient courage to initiate this process and see your personal adventure through. A person may not be born with an overabundance of talent, but he or she will certainly possess all the courage needed, whether used or unused, to develop the talent that is there. Long after passing on to the next world, we will be remembered by family and friends, not necessarily for our inborn talents, but for the amount of courage we used, especially during our times of trial. The strength and vividness of the memories our loved ones and friends hold of us after we are gone will be directly proportional to the amount of courage we have chosen to use.

Immediate Action: Starve your fear! Feed your courage! Embrace your adventure!

Point to Ponder Before You Go On: "Fear knocked at the door. Faith answered. No one was there." (From above the fireplace at Hinds' Head Hotel, near London.)

Chapter 37

Act Before the Day Is Gone!

"Change is the watchword of progression. When we tire of well-worn ways, we seek for new. This restless craving in the souls of men spurs them to climb and to seek the mountain view."
—Ella Wheeler Wilcox, American poet and journalist

What makes you feel as though you've embarked on a grand adventure in your life? We all need to be reminded of that feeling from time to time. I can remember one occasion, not too long ago, when I was reminded of it vividly.

In Salt Lake City, there's a legendary spot called Sam Weller's Bookstore. It has an enormous inventory of old and rare books. One day, I was in the checkout line with a stack of about 15 antique books. Who should happen to walk by but Mr. Weller himself! The proprietor pointed at my stack and said, "You're a collector." I acknowledged as much, and the two of us started talking about old books. Mr. Weller asked a few questions—why I collected old books (I often use them as a resource in my speaking engagements), when I got started, and which authors I collected. These include Elbert Hubbard, Orison Swett Marden, George Ade, Richard Halliburton, and a few more.

He asked me what I did for a living. I explained that I spoke at conventions, sales meetings, and seminars on leadership and personal high performance.

He thought for a moment and said, "Have you read *Light from Many Lamps?*"

I told him I hadn't. He smiled, and then he made a motion with his head, like he wanted me to step out of the checkout line.

"If you're in that kind of business," he said, "you need to take a look at page 114 in *Light from Many Lamps* by Lillian Eichler

Watson. It's an old book, a collection of quotations. I have a copy of it up on the mezzanine right over there," he said, pointing. "Let me get it for you. You don't have to buy it, but if you have time I'd like to show you page 114." By this time, I was pretty darned interested in what he had to show me.

I stepped out of the line and said, "If what you read in that book was important enough to you for you to memorize the page number, then we've got some talking to do. I'm not going to leave this store until you go up there to get *Light from Many Lamps*, so I can see what's on page 114." He smiled and walked away.

He came back down and showed me what was on page 114 of that book. I felt I understood more about the adventure that is human life than I ever had before. The moment I finished reading the passage, I knew I had to buy the volume the bookstore owner had put in my hands. Here's what I read that day in Salt Lake City; it's a passage that instantly made me think of my life as a profound joy, a great privilege, and a truly spectacular adventure. I pass it along because I believe it will have the same effect on you—and besides, I wouldn't want to keep you in suspense!

"The author views death not as the enemy of life but its friend. For it is the knowledge that our years are limited that make them so precious. It is the truth that time has been lent to us which makes us, at our best, look upon our years as a trust handed into our temporary keeping. We are like children privileged to spend a day in the great park, a park filled with many gardens and playgrounds and azure tinted lakes, with white boats sailing upon the tranquil lakes.

"True, the day allotted to each one of us is not the same in length, in light, in beauty. Some children of earth are privileged to spend a long and sunlit day in the garden here. For others the day is shorter, cloudier, and dusk descends more quickly, as in Winter's tale. But whether our life is a long summery day or a shorter wintry afternoon, we know that inevitably there are storms and squalls which overcast even the bluest heaven, and there are sunlit rays which pierce the darkest autumn sky. The day that we are privileged to spend in the great park of life is not the same for all human beings. But there is enough beauty, and joy, and gaiety in the hours if we will but treasure it.

"Then for each one of us the moment comes when the great nurse Death takes man the child by the hand and quietly says, 'It is time to

go home. Night is coming; it is your bedtime, child of earth. Come, you're tired. Lie down at last in the quiet nursery of nature and sleep. Sleep well; the Day is gone. Stars shine in the canopy of eternity.' "
—Joshua Loth Liebman, American spiritual leader

Immediate Action: Make the most of your "day" while it lasts—and launch an adventure!

Point to Ponder Before You Go On: If you're in sales, look once again at the Sam Weller story. Notice how well he knew his inventory, and how quickly and skillfully he qualified me. It didn't take him long to close that sale!

Chapter 38

Fences Were Built for Those Who Cannot Fly

"They shall mount up with wings like eagles. They shall run and not be weary. They shall walk and not faint."
—Isaiah 40:31

Adventure is the experience of reaching out and trying something new. It's praying for wings, for the ability to run and not be weary. Adventure is taking direct action toward an exciting new goal. The adventure phase of no-limits achievement is where you launch your plan and solve the problems you encounter along the way.

There are so many adventurers we can model ourselves after. In later chapters, I'll be sharing experiences that helped me to build adventure into my life on a daily basis. But I don't want you to think for a minute that I'm the ultimate role model for barrier-breaking achievement on this score, because I'm not! My own role models who have embraced ongoing adventure in life are too numerous to list here, but it's my hope that you'll become inspired to learn more about them on your own. The stories of people such as Henry Ford, Harvey Firestone, Thomas Edison, Dr. Alexis Carrel, Charles A. Lindbergh, Jim Newton, Jacques Cousteau, Walt Disney, Neil Armstrong, George S. Patton, and Wilbur and Orville Wright all have superior lessons to offer on the art of the adventurous life. Then there's a fellow named Yeager—a man who is said to have "fed off danger like a high-energy candy bar." I'll get to him in a minute.

I guess I first fell in love with adventure second hand as a spectator while growing up in Marion, Illinois, during World War II. My adventure-filled weekends consisted of a trip to each of the town's two movie theaters to see the latest John Wayne, Roy Rogers, or Gene Autry movie. That was a long time ago—back in the days when all the movie heroes were unapologetic "good guys."

That's how I first came in contact with the idea of adventure. How did you? What do you associate with this momentous word?

There are five questions you can ask to help identify exactly what the deepest adventure means to you.

What was the defining incident in your life?

Why was it defining?

How did you react to it?

Why did you react that way?

What did you learn from that reaction?

For me that "defining incident" would have to be the first time I broke the sound barrier. That moment was a long time in coming, but I know it changed me forever.

My father had been a coal miner, and before that, for a while, a wrestler—back when wrestling was still "legit." Then he owned a little neighborhood grocery store. Much as I admired the way my dad had worked hard to support my mother and me, I was convinced that I should try to do something new, something different.

I hadn't been much of an athlete in high school, but in college I played football on the line, offensive tackle and defensive center. I had to make up for my lack of size with an aggressive forearm that collected quite a few teeth over the course of my football career. Building my skills on the gridiron gave me a lot of confidence, and so did the time I spent on the college wrestling team. Much of what I learned as a wrestler—not being afraid to be out there alone, with no place to hide—came in very handy later on in life.

Getting into the Air Force, learning to fly, and working my way up to the most powerful planes—those experiences were confidence-builders, too. Every time I would crawl into the cockpit of a faster fighter, I would say, "Man, that's it! I'm never going to be able to handle this." But then after three or four flights and a few hours of flying time, I suddenly felt like I was the hottest thing in the sky. Then came the day my commanding officer said, "Okay, hotshot, this is your day to go supersonic." He was telling me that it was my day to break the sound barrier—something I'd never done before—in an airplane that was barely equipped for the task.

Faster than the speed of sound! I could remember when no one had yet broken the sound barrier. It hadn't been that long ago that people had considered the idea of exceeding the speed of sound a physical impossibility. And then a fellow by the name of Chuck Yeager came along. Suddenly everyone had a role model, a reason to be confident, a reason to take on a goal that had always seemed unattainable.

And there I was, 11 years after Yeager pushed past that seemingly unbreakable barrier, getting ready to outrace sound myself.

That's an experience I'll never forget! I strapped myself into my fighter, took off, climbed to 43,000 feet, pushed the throttle all the way up, lit the afterburner, pulled the nose up, rolled the airplane, inverted, and pulled the nose down into a 90-degree, vertical high-speed dive, pointed directly at the Okeefenokee swamp. Talk about a thrill. What a rush!

When you're diving directly at the earth you see no sky. All you see is a wall, which is the ground, coming directly at you. I cracked the sound barrier, but I didn't have much time to think about the accomplishment at the time, because I was still roaring toward that wall. I came out of afterburner, pulled back the throttle, put the speed brakes out, put both feet up on the instrument panel and pulled on the control stick like a son of a gun. I came out of that dive just about eye level to the alligators there in the swamp.

As the altimeter reversed itself, showing a gain in altitude, it dawned on me: I'd really done it; I'd broken the sound barrier. And that's when I said to myself, "I did it. I have really done something. I've done something that no one from my past ever did. I've done something that even I'm impressed with."

There were bigger adventures to follow, but the feeling of having lived through something like that was truly a life-changer. The truth is, I got addicted to it. Later on, I was flying airplanes that could go almost twice the speed of sound, airplanes that could go supersonic in a climb. These were exciting adventures, but they weren't the ultimate adventure. That's always just ahead of where we are right now.

Charles Lindbergh once wrote to his dear friend General Jimmy Dolittle (who had invited the famous pilot to a formal dinner), "Life just seems to me to be too full of things worthwhile to spend a lot of time celebrating the past...." Lindbergh knew, as all no-limits achievers do, that the ultimate adventure lies just across the threshold that marks the boundary between our developed and undeveloped potential. Old achievements are "yesterday's news." What's the new challenge, the new goal?

With discipline, we can have a little of that ultimate adventure every day. In the words of Frank Herbert, author of *Threshold: The Blue Angels Experience*, "One must learn by doing the thing. For though you think you know it, you have no certainty until you try, and at that moment you cross the threshold."

Immediate Action: Describe the defining incident in your life.

Point to Ponder Before You Go On: To paraphrase clergyman Phillips Brooks, the no-limits achiever doesn't pray for challenges equal to his current powers, but for powers equal to his next challenge!

Chapter 39

Newman's Law

"The deliberate, volitional movement out of the comfort zone."
—Definition of no-limits achievement by Jim Newman, founder of PACE Seminars

There was something one had to be keenly aware of concerning the ejection seats I used while I was in the Air Force. Basically, the pilot was strapped into a seat that was sitting on top of a 35-millimeter cannon shell. There were pluses and minuses to this arrangement. One plus was that the propulsion would lift you, in a hurry, out of any situation you felt was intolerable. A significant minus, of course, was that activating the ejection seat was a lot like suddenly being blown out into a 600-mile-per-hour wind. Not a whole lot of fun! That knowledge keeps you from activating the system for recreational purposes.

There was, however, a major problem that had to do with what some pilots did after ejecting. Let me give you a little background that will help you understand what I mean. In action movies that feature flight sequences, people always say, "Hit the ejection button!" Actually, there isn't an ejection button in a jet like the ones I flew. There are two armrests that slope down at about 45 degrees, and at the end of each one there is a metal hoop. When you lift up an armrest (either one will do the job), that blows the canopy. You now have a convertible with the top down, and you're cruising at 600 miles per hour! You reach for the trigger at the end of the armrest that initiates the ejection seat. Squeeze it. Boom! You're now out of the airplane and tumbling toward terra firma. All you have to do at this point is roll forward out of the seat, which frees up your chute and allows it to open.

The system worked great, until you plugged in the human factor. The designers found that some pilots, after having ejected, were clinging with a (literal) death grip to the armrest handles of the seat—

the last remnant of the cockpit where, before, they'd been safe. Strictly speaking, this made no sense, because everybody knows that the seat, on its own, is not an efficient shock absorber when you strike the ground at, say, 200 miles per hour. A number of pilots rode the seat all the way down to the ground—to their deaths. All they had to do was roll forward out of the seat and the parachute would open automatically at a given altitude. They didn't. The instinct to hang on to the last vestiges of a familiar surrounding, one where they'd always been safe, was a killer.

So the Air Force came up with a brilliant idea: They added a couple of new devices to the seat. One was a two-inch wide, heavy strap that went under the pilot from the front of the seat and up behind the parachute, thus placing it between the chute and the seat. This strap had a little electric take-up reel attached to it behind the headrest. One second after the seat ejected, the seat belt blew open automatically. One second after that, the take-up reel automatically took up the slack on the strap behind the pilot, instantly forming a straight line from the top of the back of the seat to the front edge of the base of the seat. This arrangement forced the pilot out of the seat—no questions asked. Not the most pleasant experience, but it sure beat plunging to your death clutching a seat that had what you might call S.A.D.—significant aerodynamic disadvantages.

The pilots called the new mechanism the "butt snapper," and the name stuck. In my leadership seminars, I have often kiddingly suggested that we need to create a device like that to put in the chair of every sales representative, manager, front-line employee, and corporate strategist who "settles in." If you see someone sitting around, wondering, out of sheer force of habit, when the action's going to get interesting, at the same time customers needed to be serviced, all you do is "hit the button." The reel takes up the slack on their butt snapper strap, and wham! That person is out of their chair.

I've asked rooms filled with senior executives, "How many of you would like such a device for your sales force?" I've seen every single hand go up. Perhaps the butt snapper is an idea whose time has come.

The truth is, when it comes time to launch our plan, we all need a butt snapper in our life. We need something that will keep us from getting a death grip on the chair where we've gotten too comfortable. We need something that will inspire us to take action—to move on.

We need to find a way to boost ourselves out of accepting comfortable situations that may have worked in the past, but are just not worth holding onto for their own sake any more. One of the best "butt snapper" routines I know of is to share your goals with your friends, co-workers, and family members. Talk about what you want to do and when you want to do it—in detail. Explain the positive aspects and the potential challenges of the things you want to accomplish, and get feedback from the people you love and respect about the plans you've established. This has two benefits. One, you'll gain new insights on the advantages and disadvantages of your plan. And two, you'll be far less likely to put off concrete action toward your goals if you've shared those goals—and their deadlines—with people you see every day.

I knew one salesperson who had her kids write down the family goals, complete with color pictures, on big posters that she placed at strategic points around the house. That's a major "butt snapper!" Your kids will remind you of what you've promised to do. Count on it.

Time for a change? Make it! Reach down, pull the trigger, and roll out. The "butt snapper" strikes again!

Immediate Action: What preconceptions or assumptions have kept you from launching your adventure in the past? What plans to overcome these former obstacles are you willing to discuss with friends and family?

Point to Ponder Before You Go On: "Thank God every morning when you get up that you have something to do that day which must be done, whether you like it or not. Being forced to work and forced to do your best will breed in you temperance, self-control, diligence, strength of will, cheerfulness, contentment, and a hundred virtues which the idle will never know."
—Charles Kingsley, English author and clergyman

Chapter 40

Launching
Your Plan

"Theorizing never put muscles in your arms or money in your pocket."
—Anonymous

"What could go wrong? And what could we do about it?" That's a question no-limits achievers frequently ask themselves. They take intelligent risks...risks that have a clear chance of a positive outcome. The people who take intelligent risks aren't reckless—they have a strong understanding of all the elements that make up the challenge they face.

When I was doing air shows, I knew that the things I was doing looked incredibly dangerous—and they were. But the pilots always planned every detail of those air shows down to the last gnat's eyelash. That's why accidents are rare in those shows. Every possible element of uncontrolled risk has been so thoroughly worked through that the plan is reliable.

The magicians Penn and Teller are noted for doing incredibly dramatic and dangerous feats for paying customers, often on a spectacular (and nerve-racking) scale. They catch speeding bullets, immerse themselves in tanks of water, and do plenty of other mind-boggling stunts, always amazing and astounding and (last but not least) amusing their audiences. It looks as though these two men are risking their lives, night after night.

At one Penn and Teller performance a friend of mine saw, there was a tiny, sharp, shiny metal object on the stage; perhaps it was a hatpin. Whatever it was, it had apparently fallen off of someone's costume. Penn (the guy who actually talks) stopped the entire performance cold. He leaned over, grabbed the small metal object, muttered "Now there's something nice and dangerous," and tossed it safely into the wings, where a stagehand retrieved it. The show had ceased for an instant as he assessed this unexpected new piece of information. That tiny hunk of metal represented a new variable, something that hadn't been planned for. Suppose someone slipped on it? Suppose someone became distracted by it? Suppose someone accidentally kicked it out into the audience?

Nothing extraneous or unplanned would be allowed to cause potential disaster during Penn and Teller's show. If the variables changed, the act stopped in its tracks.

That story puts risk-taking in a whole new perspective, doesn't it? With no-limits people, there is no such thing as risk-taking without a plan. Something may be being done for the very first time, and there may be risks associated with that undertaking, but there is always an understanding of what the downside of that risk might be.

Immediate Action: Ask yourself, "How do I feel when the plan goes into action? Am I eager to pursue the new adventure that will soon unfold? Am I ready to spot the little distractions that might derail the adventure?"

Point to Ponder Before You Go On: "He takes chances, but never leaves anything to chance."
—Jim Newton, on Charles Lindbergh

Chapter 41

Win Back Time
in Your Day

"1: Not reading long-winded reports, but only devoting attention to those that are concisely summarized. 2: Reading quickly, through continual practice; making decisions speedily; performing virtually all tasks quickly. 3: Not wasting energy reviewing decisions that have already been made–and working instead to implement decisions once they've been finalized. 4: Developing detailed knowledge of current problems. 5: Starting the day early. 6: Taking a nap at midday. 7: Refusing to worry."
—General George C. Marshall's seven habits for high-level achievement, adapted from Dale Carnegie's Biographical Roundup

"I haven't got the time."
"My schedule is packed."
"There just aren't enough hours in the day."
Do these sentiments sound familiar? Most of the people I talk to about personal time management say similar things about the way their own days unfold (or collapse!).

As we'll see a little later in this book, learning how to win back time from your day is one of the hallmarks of adventurous living. How can you "reclaim" two, three, or four hours during the day? The trick is to use the knowledge of what you would do with the extra time to motivate you to make better use of the time you have. No one can give you those extra hours a day—except you. If you're organized, you might just find that there are steps you can take that will leave you in a much better position to enjoy time with your family at the end of the day, or spend more time with great books, or get in shape, or beat that tough deadline once and for all.

It may take work to find extra hours in each day, but I believe you can do it. Those hours may not run consecutively, but they will be there, and the more motivated you are about reclaiming them to do what you want, the more likely you'll be able to win them back into your day.

Immediate Action: One way to develop your skills at time planning is to choose one hour of your day and plan how to use it most effectively. Figure out how to structure things to get the maximum amount out of that hour. At the end of the day, see how good you feel about what you accomplished during that time. The next day, plan a bigger slice. Gradually increase your planning to achieve greater and greater mastery over time instead of time having mastery over you. Remember, that you do not climb Mount Everest in a single step, but in many small steps, learned and mastered over a period of time.

Elbert Hubbard said, "You don't climb the mountain by standing in the valley and jumping over it." You have to take it a step at a time!

Point to Ponder Before You Go On: There are lots of ways to reclaim found time. Doing so may mean getting up an hour earlier or going to bed an hour later. It may mean taking a task that usually takes you an hour to do and learning to do it in 45 minutes, and then perhaps learning that you can do it in half an hour. It may even mean deciding that you aren't going to do that task any more! Perhaps it can be delegated to another person, or perhaps it doesn't even need to be done. Give yourself permission to make those decisions.

Sometimes winning back time means deciding to take some things out of our lives that are nice, but that are just too time-consuming. In our garden, we used to have some very prolific roses in a corner planter. They were tremendously hardy. Weather, wind, drought, insects, nothing bothered them. I used to spend about three hours every Saturday, just pruning off the spent blossoms. Then one day I decided to replace the roses with the kind of plants we had in other parts of the garden that were equally beautiful, but that required much less upkeep. Now I spend no more than 30 minutes a week on that part of the garden and I have 2 1/2 extra hours each Saturday to appreciate the garden...or do other things!

Chapter 42

The Inner Cave

"Concerning all acts of creation, there is one elementary truth ... that the moment one definitely commits oneself, then Providence moves too."
—Goethe

Sometimes, you can hear an adventure saying, "Dive in—and don't stop swimming until you get where you mean to go!" My wife and I were on a Blue Lagoon cruise a few years ago, going up through the Yasawa Islands north of Fiji. These are tiny, remote islands with very small populations and no roads. One crew member said that if anyone wanted him to, he could take us to a very small, very special cave.

This, it turned out, was an inner cave connected to the outside by a tube. The only way to reach the cave was by going underwater with only the air in your lungs. It was a beautiful "natural room," with plenty of air, but it was only accessible by swimming through the underwater tube. It was quite an exhilarating experience to duck your head and swim through that tube, knowing you had to go all the way in one effort. An experience like that can be a real character builder! There was no turning back halfway, no stopping for rest. Was it a barrier—or a test?

Some special "rooms" are like that. To reach them, you have to know where you're going, you have to know what the plan is for getting there, and know that the path you've chosen has a fair chance of success. (We didn't plunge into an underwater passageway with no idea where it led! If we'd wanted to do that, we would have needed different equipment—a scuba outfit, for instance—and a new set of strategies.)

I think there are plenty of special events in life that require the kind of committed effort I'm talking about. Whether you're trying to land the right job, meet an ambitious sales quota, or develop a proposal that will win an important new client for your firm, it's important to recognize a situation that requires a deep breath, a plunge forward, and continued, unremitting effort—no matter what—until you reach your goal.

Immediate Action: Sit down and think about your goals. What goal have you set for yourself that will require constant, unremitting effort? What's the first step in achieving that barrier-breaking goal? The second? The third? The fourth? Remember, they don't have to be large steps, but they do have to take you closer to your ultimate goal.

Point to Ponder Before You Go On: When you are up against a seemingly impossible problem en route to your goal, there's a very good chance that you are on the brink of a great discovery. This kind of situation is exactly where great discoveries have historically arisen.

Chapter 43

BBDB!

"A smooth sea never develops a skillful sailor."
—Ancient proverb

To make it through challenges when you're turning your plan into reality, you have to follow the BBDB rule: Bend but don't break! (When you're bending, you're generally learning what doesn't work, which is just as important as learning what does work.)

When I was based in the Philippines, I was sent to Water Survival School in Japan. The idea was to learn how to survive if you found yourself parachuting into the ocean after "opening the door and leaving the building"—ejecting from your plane. I told myself that, if that ever happened to me, I wanted to learn how to live, to survive, no matter what. As it turned out, that was a commitment I actually questioned during the seven-day training program.

The warmest it ever got at the spot where we had this training was 57 degrees free air temperature, which meant that things could get very chilly, especially when you were soaking wet all day. One of the survival tests involved dropping us off individually for four hours, several miles out into the Sea of Japan, in a one-man "dinghy" like the one we had in our survival kits that made up the cushion or our ejection seats. It was tiny!

How did the training work? First, I jumped off the back of a speeding boat from a 15-foot platform. My parachute harness was attached to the boat, which meant that I was immediately body surfing—on my back. While I was being dragged behind the boat, I had to reach up and release both sides of the parachute harness at the same time. If I released only one side, I knew I would immediately start "corkscrewing" through the water. This is not good. Whirling around in the water can fill up your lungs with sea water. I concentrated very hard on executing those harness releases at exactly the same time. Fortunately, I was successful.

Next, I had to inflate the individual dinghy attached to the remaining part of my parachute harness. When I say this was an "individual" dinghy, I'm telling the truth; it was extremely individual. Short as my legs are, I still couldn't sit with them stretched out. This was a very tiny piece of lifesaving equipment, but I soon learned that it did float, as advertised.

So there I was—left to bob around on the Sea of Japan for four hours (or so I was told), out of sight of land or any of my fellow "survivors," all by myself. I remember spending the first hour and a half wondering whether this was really what I had signed on to do in the service of my country.

The four hours passed. By that point I had had plenty of time for patriotic introspection, and had moved on to new subjects. Now I was trying to figure out exactly how much fun it was to be cold, bored, suffering from exposure, and seasick, all at the same time. I was just about to make my final conclusions on the matter when the rescue boat appeared on the horizon.

As you can imagine, I was excited to see that boat. It was impossible to stand up on the dinghy, so I shouted and waved with all the enthusiasm I could muster. But the boat kept its (considerable) distance, went right on by, and disappeared again over the horizon. And there I was, all alone again.

Hours went by, no boat. Five hours, then six hours, then seven hours alone in that extremely individual dinghy was way more than I had bargained for, especially since I had a sneaking suspicion that I was now lost at sea, and that the Air Force might not ever be back to look for me again. How much fun, I wondered, would it really be to end my life story here?

That, I realized, was a downright demoralizing—and dangerous—thought. Sitting there on my little dinghy, I made a decision. There was no point, I reasoned, in assuming the worst about my situation. All that would do would be to keep me focused on the most *negative* aspect of the challenge I faced. I told myself that, tired and cold and seasick though I was, from that moment forward, I would assume that my ride would show up. If I was right, I'd make my time alone more bearable. If I was wrong, I'd at least be focusing on something pleasant out there in the middle of the ocean. So I thought about the boat showing up and about how glad I'd be once it did. By running those thoughts through my mind over and over again, I was able to lift my spirits quite a bit.

Well, as you've probably already gathered, the Air Force didn't let me down. They finally sent a boat my way. I won't pretend that that personalized eight-hour ocean cruise was the best recreational time I've ever spent, but it did teach me an important lesson. Even when things look grim, thinking about the worst thing that could possibly happen eats up too much of your energy.

Immediate Action: Think of a time when you were in a tough spot, but you decided to focus on the positive and managed to make it through all right. The moral: Don't run failure movies in your head, only run success movies!

Point to Ponder Before You Go On: "Self-reverence, self-knowledge, self-control—these three alone lead to sovereign power." —Alfred, Lord Tennyson

Chapter 44

Your Morale Check

"The time to be happy is now; the place to be happy is here; the way to be happy is to make others so."
—Robert Ingersoll, early 20th-century author and orator

How can you tell when your own morale is dropping? Simple. If you're not having fun, recognize that you've got a problem and that you need to address it with as much care, attention, and dedication as you would any other business dilemma.

If you come home at the end of the day and say, "Whew, I made some more money, but it sure wasn't any fun," guess what? You've got a tiger by the tail. You can't keep that routine up indefinitely without running yourself down.

As we said back home, it's okay to have a tiger by the tail if you know what to do next. Take a good hard look at the point you've reached and give yourself a break. Take a step back and say, "I have to prioritize things. I have to identify the most important step I can take to solve this problem." It might be changing your workload, or taking on a new project, or setting a new goal for your company, or even, with the right planning, starting a whole new career. But if the work you're doing isn't energizing you, you need to find a way to change your focus so it does—and you need to act fast, because maintaining your own morale is a high-priority assignment!

After all, if *you're* not committed to finding a way to actually enjoy yourself during the day, who will be?

The attitude you choose to maintain as you face your challenge is all-important. Find someone whose example you can follow on this score, someone who manages to turn challenge into chuckles. My mentor and "uncommon friend," Jim Newton, has often been described as "the talking, laughing man." It's an apt description of his life style, because Jim is always talking and always laughing. No wonder those five great figures of the 20th century included him in their circle of friendship.

In so many areas, I have made a conscious effort to mirror Jim's joyous approach to life and work. One of his neatest tricks is hogtying the English language when he feels that doing so will give him (and others) an emotional lift. That's an endearing, effective way to change a "bad day" into a day of gratitude and joy.

Jim developed the habit of using "fun words." He's always trying to find a way to build fun into the day. He usually succeeds. Jim talks about the condominiums he developed as "pandamoniums," and speaks of taking advantage of "opporchancity," not opportunity. An automobile is never a car—it's a "boiler" or a "chariot." When addressing male friends, he uses words such as "Monsoor" or "Skipper." When he's concluding a conversation, he's likely to say, "Three cheers" or even, "Hang onto your hat!"

Jim takes direct personal control of his vocabulary. He uses the words he speaks (and thinks) to manage his outlook, to control the way he looks at the challenges that life brings his way. We could all do a lot worse than to follow his example.

Immediate Action: Ponder the following Jim Newtonisms—and ask yourself whether you could use expressions like these during the course of the day to help your outlook.

"What do we care for expenses? We have lots of them."

"Do you file your nails or throw them away?"

"Where there's a will, there are relatives."

(At the beginning of a letter:) "Enclosed please find 10 dollars. I can't!"

"He who hesitates is bossed."

"Something just crossed what I laughingly call my mind."

"I follow one rule without fail: Share an idea quickly, before it dies of solitary confinement!"

"I can't say much for my past—but my future is spotless!"

Point to Ponder Before You Go On: If you're regularly feeling stressed and unhappy about what you do for most of the day, you owe it to yourself to strategize a new way of living. No one else will, or can, do that for you.

Chapter 45

"But I'm Just a Little Off Course!"

"There comes a time in the affairs of men when you must take the bull by the tail and face the situation."
—W.C. Fields

An adventure is something to which you give your all. On some adventures, you have no alternative but to give your all if you wish to survive! If the mission you're on isn't important enough for you to try to complete it at a superior level of performance, then it's worth asking yourself whether it's important enough for you to take on in the first place.

This is not to say that you should expect absolute perfection from yourself (or anyone else) as you work toward your goal; there will be setbacks and mistakes along the way. But the attitude you take toward those setbacks and mistakes will say a lot about the way you're looking at the work before you. If you're trying to make great things happen, but you're operating from a "get-through-the-day" point of view, you're going to be in for some disappointments. That's the lowest level of motivation—the compliance level.

I remember when this lesson registered most dramatically for me. It was while I was still in pilot training. During one flight, my instructor took a look at his instruments and said, "You need a correction; you're off course." I checked the instruments. The pilot was right. I was one degree off.

I set the correct course, but I tried to make light of the situation. "I wasn't off by much—just one degree," I said. Later, when we were on the ground, the pilot sat me down and made me figure out exactly what that "one degree" would mean over the course of a flight of 300 miles. If I'd left that "small" error unattended, we could have ended up in the wrong time zone, looking for a runway that wasn't going to materialize. I realized I had been trying to justify "compliance-level" work. (There are three levels of motivation: compliance, goal identification, and commitment.)

A few years ago, a Japan Air Lines pilot on a flight from Tokyo to San Francisco made a similar miscalculation. Thanks to language difficulties in communications with the tower, the captain brought his airplane down just short of the runway he'd been assigned. If you're keeping score at home, you'll be interested to know what that translates to: He made a perfect water landing just short of the runway in San Francisco Bay! Fortunately, no one was injured. Later, when discussing the landing with reporters, the pilot offered an interesting justification for the landing: "Considering that I traveled all the way from Tokyo, I didn't miss by much." That's either the best backhanded "tongue-in-cheek" acknowledgment of a problem I've ever heard—or a world-champion attempt at justifying compliance-level thinking!

Immediate Action: Think of a time when you rose above "compliance level," improved your skills, and reaped a reward as a result. Replay that "success movie." It gives your morale a boost instantly.

Point to Ponder Before You Go On: If you were to stay on your current course in your job or life style, what would life look like a year from now? Five years from now? Twenty years from now? If you don't like what you see, it's time for a course change!

Chapter 46

Adventure: "We Need a Daddy"

"Life is either a daring adventure or nothing. To keep our faces toward change and behave like free spirits in the presence of fate is strength undefeatable."
—Helen Keller

Sometimes embarking on your own unique adventure means committing yourself to a new course of action with the faith, commitment, and trust of a child. Sometimes pursuing your adventure means following your own heart where it leads you. I learned that from the path that brought me to my wife, Theo, and her daughters, who became my daughters. Talk about a big adventure!

Let me explain. When I was single and flying fighters out of Tucson, the Air Force informed us, in July, that they were going to close up the squadron. I had initially been assigned to go to Columbus, Ohio, later in the year. In August they told me they were changing my assignment to Oscoda, Michigan. I had just spent the last six years, on my last two assignments, in the Philippines and in Tucson, and I was dreading leaving such warm climates for the chill of the upper Midwest. But when I called some of my buddies in Michigan, they said, "This place isn't so bad. One of the hidden benefits of this part of Michigan is that it turns into a real party town for singles in the summer, so for three months out of the year this place is great." That seemed appealing, but as August turned into October with my departure date still a couple of months off, I decided I was not excited about taking the assignment in Michigan. As if I had a choice!

Did you ever have that feeling, deep in the pit of your stomach, that you needed to make a change in order to follow your destiny? That's a voice I've learned to listen to over the years. I heard it that fall in Arizona, though I'm not sure I would have identified what I was experiencing as "intuition." I came up with all kinds of reasons to explain my desire to get back to where they told me I was going to go first. I just kept hearing that clear voice inside saying, "Go to Columbus—no matter what." Well, I listened. I wanted to go to where I had been assigned in July—Columbus, Ohio.

So, the first week in October, I walked into my commander's office and said, "You owe me a favor." It was true—he did. I had been the public relations (PR) officer and had gotten his picture in the newspapers and on television a great deal. He'd picked up quite a bit of positive attention, both on and off the base, as a result of my efforts.

"Christmas needs to come a little early this year," I said. "I don't want to go to Michigan."

He leaned back in his chair. "Well, where do you want to go?" he said.

"I want to go to my original assignment in Columbus, Ohio."

After casting a jaundiced eye over the Captain's bars on my shoulder he said, "You know, we have this little tradition in the military. It's quaint, but it's something we've come to count on. When you get an assignment, you go."

"I know," I said, "but I just don't want to go to Michigan."

"Well, why was going to Michigan a good plan from August to October," he asked, "but suddenly not a good plan now?"

"I don't know." I said. "I just know that I have to go to Columbus."

He stared at me. I knew that look on the face of a colonel; it was the look they get when there's about to be a funeral on your street, and you aren't going to be hearing the music.

"If I change your assignment," my commander warned, "you don't know for sure where you're going to end up. You could get sent to Fargo, North Dakota—you could even wind up in Reykjavik or at Thule Air Base." (Those last two outposts, in Iceland and Greenland, respectively, are considered classic "blue nose" bases in the Air Force.) "And by the way," he went on, "Columbus in the winter isn't exactly Palm Springs, Cox. What on earth are you trying to do here?"

Every instinct should have told me to snap to, concede defeat, and inform the commander that I'd go where I'd been assigned. But for some reason, I couldn't. My instincts were pointing me toward Ohio, and they were growing stronger with every passing minute.

"I'm not sure, sir, but all I can tell you is that you have to get it changed," I said. "I want to go to Columbus, Ohio."

"I can't promise you that," he said.

"I know you can get it changed for me."

He grumbled and said something about doing his best. I left his office and took off on an intercept training mission I'd been scheduled for. An hour and 15 minutes later, I was in the equipment room hanging up my parachute and crash helmet and I saw him coming down the hall looking at me through the little rectangular window pane in the door. I said to myself, "He's got something for me that is going to change my life from here on." I sensed it!

When he walked in he said, "Well, I got your assignment changed."

"Fantastic!" I was grinning from ear to ear.

"How do you know it's fantastic?" he asked. "You don't know where you're going."

"Yes I do; I'm going to Columbus, Ohio."

He tried to prolong the suspense, but it was no use. I knew full well what the piece of paper he held in his hand said.

"All right, you lucky son of a gun, you're right. It's Columbus." He smiled a little, handed me the sheet, and then turned and walked away.

Three months later I got to Columbus, Ohio, and moved into Kingsrowe Court. The week before, a young woman named Theo Walker had moved into the neighborhood. She and her three young daughters lived across the street from me. I found out from a friend in the squadron that her husband had been killed while flying a mission in Vietnam on the second of October—that is, during the very week in October when I had sensed that I had to go to Columbus, Ohio.

I now realize that this was an example of what author Don Osgood calls (in his book on the subject) "God's silent language." In this case, it was a guiding force or higher purpose seeing to it that I got the encouragement I needed to wind up where I was supposed to be, at the time I was supposed to be there. I think God talks to all of us about such things, maybe a lot more than we realize.

At the time, though, in January, in Ohio, all I could tell for sure was that I had a very attractive young widow for a neighbor—at least from what I could see through my frost-covered living room window.

I concentrated my efforts on spending as much time indoors as possible. You don't go outside to socialize much in Columbus, Ohio, in January. It didn't help that that month was one of the coldest in memory—we had sub-zero weather for what seemed like the entire month of January. After Tucson and the Philippines, I wasn't used to that kind of treatment! It took until March for it to warm up enough for me to get outdoors and work on my Corvette.

Finally! Springtime, or a convincing approximation of it. The time of year when a young man's thoughts turn to sports car maintenance. I was under the hood one fine afternoon when a little cherub from across the street made her way into my driveway. It was Theo's middle daughter—she was only five years old at the time.

"Hi, what's your name?" she asked.

"I'm Danny," I offered.

"My name's Kendra." She flashed a big grin. "Do you have a mommy?"

Assuming she meant "wife," I answered, "No."

"Well, I don't have a daddy, and my mommy lives right there," she pointed. Talk about taking the direct approach! This little girl was a born salesperson if ever there was one.

A few minutes later, Theo came out and said, "I hope my daughter hasn't been asking you any questions you couldn't handle."

"Oh, no," I said. I remember thinking to myself, "Well, here's a pretty good sales manager. Send your kid out to work the streets: "Go find us a daddy today." Then you follow up with that innocent "kids-say-the-darnedest-things" approach afterward.

I had to wonder about the possible repercussions of starting up a relationship with a woman who lived across the street from me, but we went out on a couple of platonic dates. I concluded that I should try to fix this beautiful young woman up with some other guys. I did just that, but for some reason, I always found myself standing at the living room window late in the evening staring across the street, saying to myself, "Doesn't she know what a creep that guy is yet?" Every time I found myself thinking that way, I had to stop short and ask myself, "Wait a minute. Why should I care?" After about the third or fourth time I found myself anxious on this late-night watch, that little voice inside me started talking again: "Isn't this interesting—that you find yourself so concerned over why she isn't home yet?"

Before long, she and I began talking about a great many things. We began to sense that there was something special between us. Eventually, of course, we figured out that we were in love. We decided that we would get married in November, which was a little more than 13 months after her first husband had been killed in action. We had to plan carefully how we would tell everybody. We decided we would tell her parents first. Then we would call his parents, as they were still very much a part of the lives of Theo and her kids (and were so until their deaths many years later). Then we would tell the squadron.

I realized that that was going to be an interesting process. This sort of situation can be tricky in a flight squadron. There were 60-plus flight crew members, and their wives. All those couples would be standing shoulder to shoulder to protect Theo from wild fighter pilots like me. Fortunately, everyone respected our decision and understood how carefully Theo and I had considered matters before making our commitment to each other.

Lastly, we planned to tell the three girls. (We knew that if we told them about our intentions any earlier, we'd quickly lose control of our information!) Then came the big day. After a last-minute conversation, we decided that I would walk across the street to my apartment, and Theo would tell them. She would give them a chance to ask all the questions they wanted to ask—what having me as a daddy was going to be like, the fact that I had never had children, all those things. Then she would call me on the phone to come over and join the family. They were to take whatever time it took. If she didn't call me until the next morning, that was okay—the girls were to have the option to take as long as they needed to deal with this new event in their lives.

So I walked across the two-lane street. As I reached my door, the phone began to ring. I went inside and picked it up; it was Theo. Not 45 seconds had passed since I'd left her at her door. "Come on back," she said.

I remember thinking to myself that this could be either very good or very bad.

"What happened?" I asked.

"Just come on back," she said.

"Did you tell the kids?"

"Yes," she said.

"Give me an idea of what their reaction was."

"Just come on back," she said. And hung up!

So as I walked back across the street I had crossed just a minute or two before, I was trying to remember whether or not it was good or bad for you when the jury reaches a quick decision.

I opened the door and walked into the living room. Kendra (six by this time) came bounding across the room. In addition to being a champion daddy finder, she is also the family gymnast. She leapt up and threw her arms around my neck.

"I know something," she whispered excitedly in my ear.

"What do you know?" I teased.

"You're going to marry us!"

Something deep inside told me she'd known it for a while—and that, somehow, I had, too.

The adventure had begun. Like all worthwhile adventures, it had begun with a whisper of an idea and had grown into something tangible because someone believed in it enough to make it a reality. Like all worthwhile adventures, it took a little courage to begin, but it felt intuitively right at the moment of commitment. Like all worthwhile adventures, it opened up the participants to a whole new world of previously unimagined possibilities. It's a dream of an adventure that has been going on for 33 years now!

Children live those kinds of adventures on a daily basis. Grownups need to make sure they don't miss out on the adventures they're meant to enjoy, too.

Immediate Action: Ask yourself: When was the last time you heard a voice, deep inside, telling you to take a particular course of action? What did you do? What do you wish you'd done? Will you listen more intently when you hear that voice again?

Point to Ponder Before You Go On: Barrier-breakers understand that they sometimes have to tell themselves, "I've circled the mountain long enough. It's time to start up."

Chapter 47

What Is Courage?

"Bravery is being terrified, but saddling up anyway."
—John Wayne

I believe that it is everyone's sacred duty to be prepared to do the biggest thing possible that needs to be done at any given moment. That's not to say that doing the big thing is always easy—but doing the big thing is always necessary.

The legendary actor Hume Cronyn once told a story about meeting Orson Welles in the late 1930s: "I was lunching at Sardi's one day and Orson came over to say hello. I had just seen his *Julius Caesar*. He had given it in modern dress. It was the only time I had seen that work as a comment on fascism, and [it was] very stirring. I said to Orson, 'What I admired about your production is your sheer courage.' 'Courage?' [Welles replied.]...'Courage! That's going to the edge—because you have to be good.'"

Going to the edge can be scary, but it's a consistent habit of no-limits achievers. As you approach a self-imposed barrier, you may hear a voice saying, "This far and no farther." It's not the barrier's voice that you hear. Listen carefully. Do you recognize it? It's your own!

Immediate Action: The next time you feel fear in pursuing a goal, ask yourself, "Am I listening to my fear or my courage?" Either choice can become a habit.

Point to Ponder Before You Go On: If you don't summon the courage necessary to take care of a problem, the problem may take care of you!

Chapter 48

The Biggest
Mistakes

"It's as though we spend years learning the names of the cards without learning to play the game."
—Robert Ingersoll, early 20th-century author and orator

I ngersoll was right. Let the game begin! Once the game of life starts, no-limits achievers commit themselves to playing it as well as they possibly can. Take a look at the chart on the following page for some classic mistakes—errors that are well worth learning to avoid once we've committed ourselves to "playing" with full attention and effort.

Immediate Action: Photocopy the list on the following page and keep it at your desk, where you can see it every day.

Point to Ponder Before You Go On: There's nothing wrong with making a mistake once, as long as you learn enough from it to avoid repeating it in the future.

The Biggest Mistakes

Orison Swett Marden once identified 14 great human mistakes. He felt it was a great mistake for us to:

1. Set our own standard of right and wrong.
2. Judge people accordingly.
3. Measure the joy of others by our own.
4. Expect uniformity of opinion in this world.
5. Look for judgment or experience in youth.
6. Endeavor to mold all dispositions alike.
7. Yield to immaterial trifles.
8. Look for perfection in our own actions.
9. Worry ourselves and others with what cannot be remedied.
10. Fail to alleviate all that needs alleviation so far as lies in our power.
11. Fail to make allowance for the infirmities of others.
12. Consider everything impossible that we cannot perform.
13. Believe only what our finite minds can grasp.
14. Expect to be able to understand everything.

Chapter 49

Perspective Makes the Difference

"We acquire the strength of the thing we have overcome."
—Ralph Waldo Emerson

We all know that life is full of challenging situations. The question is, how do we respond to them? With fear or with full, confident attention?

On the supersonic fighters I flew, we had a big yellow "master caution light" at the top of the instrument panel, where you could see it easily. When that thing came on it meant you needed to look down at the "idiot panel" and see which "idiot light" was lit up—indicating which major system had gone wrong. The point was to pay real close attention to what the lights were telling you and react in a specific way.

We need to have a similar "master caution light" for ourselves—a light that's flipped on by our own intuition. This kind of intuition is a spin-off of being highly motivated, and that motivation, in turn, comes about as a result of seeing what you want really good in your mind, à la George Foreman, and committing your strength totally to achieving your goal. Once you do that, intuition kicks in and goes to work on figuring out what new problems you're going to run into. It also helps you prepare for those problems.

We need the light of our own intuition to go off and remind us to check over all the little details that may be going wrong unnoticed—details that will eventually reach up and bite us if we're not careful. Checking the master caution light is one of the things you need to be sensitive to when you check how you feel at the end of the day. It's essentially the same thing as asking yourself, "Have I overlooked something important?" and listening carefully to what you hear in response.

If that master caution light is on, go back through the day and check to see which problem areas are lit up, so you can give them the attention they need.

We all have problems. The trick, as Oliver Wendell Holmes once observed, is to learn to look at a problem as a challenge—and not as an opportunity to win sympathy from others. One of the best ways to do this is to remind yourself of the true dimensions of the challenge you face.

Barrier-breakers learn not to self-dramatize when they find themselves in a tough fix. They don't send themselves the wrong messages: "I've blown it!" "How on earth do I get out of this one?" "I can't possibly solve this!"

If you really are in a tight spot, you have too much real work to do to keep those messages playing. You don't have time to editorialize like that.

So often someone comes up to me after one of my talks and says, "Danny, I'm in a terrible situation. I have to talk to you." I ask them, "Is this the worst situation you have ever been in in your whole life?" The object is to make them stop and think.

"No," they usually reply. "This is nothing compared to that."

"Well," I say, "if we walk you through this with that perspective, you should get through this one a lot quicker."

I'm not suggesting you dwell on the worst experience you've ever had, just that you remind yourself of it from time to time and use it to help keep things in perspective. I know what I compare my own "challenging" days with. It was a winter flight that got a little toastier than I'd anticipated.

One stormy January day, my radar observer, Pete Gillespie, and I took off for Michigan from Columbus, Ohio. As we lifted off, I grabbed the landing gear handle and brought it up in a split second. This airplane's 79,000 horsepower could accelerate you past the maximum "landing gear down" speed in a hurry. As soon as the gear came up the defrosters kicked in. That puzzled me because I thought I had inadvertently skipped the switch in my preflight check, and that it had therefore been left on from a previous flight.

The defrosters on a plane like the one I was flying bring air straight in from the engine—as opposed to the ones on your car, which work off a small heating coil. That air shoots into the cockpit at more than 200 degrees. Even though it mixes with the ambient air, the hot air can make the cockpit hotter than...well, hotter than you'd like it to be. So you try not to keep the defrosters running any longer than you have to.

In a few minutes, I noticed that the cockpit was getting very warm. I reached down, meaning to flip the switch to the "off" position. But it was already off.

There was some sort of malfunction, and whatever it was, it was dumping some very hot air into my cockpit. There was no way to control the temperature. There we were, flying in a terrible winter storm—turbulence, snow, ice, sleet, and wind. It was a really terrible weather situation outside, but we had bigger problems inside the plane. We had a tropical heat wave (times 50) going on in the cockpit, and I had to figure out what to do.

I called the control center and explained that I had a "Mayday" situation. I decided that we weren't going to go on to Michigan after all; we wanted to go back to where we had taken off from, as soon as possible. We found a clear spot and got permission from air traffic control to go down to a lower altitude, where I could burn fuel more quickly and prepare for our return to Columbus. (Landing on an icy runway with all the fuel we were carrying could have been very dangerous, because of the increased landing speed necessary to offset the excess weight—approximately four tons needed to be burned.) In the meantime, all of this heat was pouring into the cockpit, making it so hot that I had trouble thinking—hotter than any sauna I could imagine.

When I got down to the lower altitude, I went into a 360-degree turn and played a little trick to get rid of fuel so that I could prepare to land. By lighting the afterburner, then shutting it off and immediately putting the throttles back in to afterburner position, the "burners" would not relight—but the extra fuel that was being sent back would continue to pour out the tailpipe. It's the poor man's way of dumping fuel.

Suddenly my eyes started to water as the cockpit filled with smoke and burning paint fumes. The defroster couldn't handle the heat, either. It was burning itself out. I knew that feeling; Pete and I were really getting dehydrated—we'd passed the point of perspiring! At this point, I was considering "blowing" the canopy so I could avoid passing out from the heat, but the severe weather made landing without the canopy the kind of bet Mrs. Cox didn't raise her boy

Danny to put money on. The sauna in the cockpit kept blazing away.

I burned the fuel way down and then checked in with the air base where I wanted to land. My aim was to get a straight vector in to the runway. This was a crisis, and everybody knew it. I asked for a GCA. Officially, GCA stands for "Ground Control Approach," but this kind of improvised instruction delivery is often known by pilots as a "Gonna Crash Anyway" situation. Basically, GCA means the people on the ground have to come up with the right answer, and fast, for the pilot—and the pilot has to hope they're right as they line him up with the runway and talk him down the glide slope they see on their radar.

My GCA controller told me that they had had an abrupt reversal of the wind, which meant landing from the opposite direction than normal. They were busy recomputing and retuning everything, and they couldn't give me the information I needed for landing yet. My eyes were beginning to hurt; the tears were making it hard to see. Fortunately, breathing wasn't a problem, because we had our oxygen masks on.

Finally, GCA started lining us up for the landing. We were "in the soup"—the clouds, we were told, extended almost to the ground. They talked me down the glide slope to "minimums," which meant if we weren't out of the clouds by that very low altitude, we'd have to execute a "go around" and try again. Suddenly we broke out of the clouds, but no runway was ahead of us. It was about 150 yards to the left. It turned out our heading indicator was also a casualty. This was not *going* to be one of those days—*it was* one of those days.

It was time for the Test Pilot's Prayer that I had already learned to say very quickly: "Okay, God, get this thing on the ground, and I'll taxi it in for you!" I pushed the throttles forward and pulled up into the clouds—so near and yet so far.

"We'll take over," ground control said. "We'll tell you when to turn and how many degrees to bank the turn; we'll tell you when to roll out." I followed their instructions carefully. I was flying blind in the storm, praying the voices from ground control would get me around the pattern, bring me down once again, and put a long, beautiful runway in front of me.

On the second approach, just as I reached the point at which I had to break clear and be able to see—or else pull up and go back around again—I broke clear of the clouds. I could make out my position, all right: This time, I was only about 100 yards to the right. I immediately executed a 90-degree turn to the left, which is difficult to do at less than a hundred feet of altitude with landing gear, flaps, and speed brakes out. I can remember seeing the controllers diving out of the ground-control shack at the end of the runway. They thought I was going to give them a "fly-through" rather than a "fly-by"! Then I executed another 90-degree turn, this time to the right, and lined up with the runway.

By this time, though, we were way too far down the runway to land. If I'd tried to touch down, I'd have run off the end of the runway at high speed—not a good idea, especially since I'd been promising myself that the day was only going to get better once I committed myself to land.

You remember what we used to say back home: "If you ain't got a choice, be brave." I had no choice but to pull up and go around again and try for another approach. It is very dicey to try to do another GCA; there are so many subtle adjustments that need to be made. But I followed all the instructions they gave me. The good news was that it was now getting cooler in the cockpit, because the defroster was now in Defroster Heaven.

I was now dangerously low on fuel, and beginning to wish I hadn't dumped quite so much of it. I had just enough fuel for one more very tight pass. I called GCA: "If I don't make it in this time, give me a clear vector to a sparsely populated area, and we'll eject." So I came around again. This time, while we were still in the clouds, they told me I was too far left for a safe approach, and that I had to turn right.

I didn't do it. They repeated, "You're too far to the left for a safe approach, turn right immediately!" I still couldn't see the runway, but based on the last two tries, I thought, "I am probably going to be just about right. I'm going to go with my gut feeling and chance it and stay right here."

That was one of those times when you have to make an instant decision about whether to go with the advice you are getting or with your own feelings. Fortunately for me and my radar observer, I had a moment of clarity at the very moment I had a choice to make. Once I made it, I knew there were three possible outcomes: In five seconds, I would be on the runway, hanging in a parachute, or dead. I was voting for the runway option; it was my clear favorite. I was definitely not looking forward to ejecting from the plane, and I know my radar observer wasn't, either—but if it came down to ejecting or Option Three, there really wasn't much choice.

As we popped out of the cloud cover, the runway was right in front of us. I touched down, and just as I taxied off the runway, the engine shut down by itself. There was not a drop of fuel left.

Talk about a low margin for error! If I'd contented myself with wasting time and energy reviewing what was "awful" about what surrounded us at any point in that experience, I would have sunk us. Fortunately, complaining never made it to the top of my list. In some situations, you just plain don't have time to bellyache.

That's my "this-too-shall-pass" story. If I'd ever come any closer to crashing, you wouldn't be reading this book. When times get tough and things look low, I ask myself, "Well, is this as bad as that 'off-the-chart' sauna I took in the cockpit?" I have yet to hear myself answer, "Yes!" I figured if I could make it through that, I could make it through just about anything. So far, I haven't been proved wrong.

Immediate Action: We all have a tendency to look at the problem we're experiencing as the biggest ever, until we stop and think about how accurate that assessment really is. The next time you're facing a major challenge, ask yourself, "Is this situation the worst one I've ever faced? How do the problems I'm facing now compare with the biggest problems I've ever encountered?" If the challenge in the past was larger—and this is usually the case—then acknowledging that will help you put things in perspective. You'll no doubt get through this difficulty far more quickly.

Point to Ponder Before You Go On: You can't solve the problem—or even address it—if you're busy convincing yourself that you're doomed.

Solving the Problem

"Don't fight forces—use them."
—Buckminster Fuller, American architect and engineer

Back home, when I was a boy, there was a strange fellow named Ticky. Everyone in town knew Ticky well. He was pleasant enough, but the truth was that he wasn't going to win any awards for brilliance. The townsfolk used to say that Ticky was a few cards shy of a full deck. His pages weren't bound quite straight. There were a few stairways in his building that didn't really lead anywhere, if you know what I mean.

People still talk about the afternoon when Ticky meandered into Orie Hiffle's blacksmith shop. Before Ticky walked in, Orie had pulled a horseshoe from the fire and set it on his anvil before moving on to work on something else. That horseshoe wasn't red-hot, but it was pretty close to it. Ticky, always curious about his surroundings, made the mistake of picking up that horseshoe with his bare hand. It didn't take him long to realize that he'd picked up something he really shouldn't have. Ticky howled and hurled the horseshoe back at the anvil.

"Ah, Ticky," Orie asked, "did that burn you?"

Ticky quickly answered, "No, it just don't take me long to look at a horseshoe!"

That's a great comeback—once! No matter how snappy our words may be, though, the truth is that we haven't learned the lesson if we keep picking up the same old hot horseshoe. Sometimes, to avoid picking up a horseshoe twice, you have to be willing to stare a problem in the face and say, "What's not working here?"

When I was selling real estate for a large corporation, I lost a big sale—one that I had worked very hard to clinch. My buddy and mentor Jim Raco heard what had happened and decided he and I ought to talk about this setback. One afternoon, he sauntered over to my desk and asked me, "How much commission did you lose on that transaction that just fell apart?"

"I don't want to think about it," I said.

"Come on, Danny. How much commission did you lose?"

"I'm not kidding, Jim," I told him. "I just spent two whole weeks working like a dog on that deal, and I didn't make a penny on it. I'd really rather not total up the losses right now."

"I know you'd rather not, but that's what you're about to do," he said, pushing a yellow legal pad and a pen my way. "Take a minute now and figure out what your commission would have been on that sale."

Well, I could tell he wasn't going to leave me alone until I did what he asked, so I picked up the pen and started doing the math. I figured out that my commission would have come to about $1,200, which, at that time, when I was just getting started in the business world, was a fair sum of money.

"Okay," he said, "you just paid a $1,200 tuition. It's time to learn the lesson. Where did it go wrong? What exactly did you do that you shouldn't have done?"

Suddenly, I was supremely motivated to find out where I'd messed up. Jim was right; I had just invested $1,200 in a lesson, and at that price, I deserved to find out what that lesson was. I started talking about questions I should have asked, research I should have done, changes I should have made in my presentation. After each new point I raised, Jim said, "Write it down."

After about 10 minutes of analyzing The Sale That Wasn't, Jim had me look over each of the items I'd jotted down on that yellow legal pad. "Now ask yourself," he said, "are you ever going to let yourself make these mistakes again?"

"No," I said. I was looking at Jim, but I was making a promise to myself. I was excited about this *lesson*! That "what-did-you-learn" question is a technique I've used many times since then.

Sometimes people embrace the fact that something went wrong and try to attribute what happened to imaginary reasons—bad luck, a down market, personality mismatches, whatever—so they don't have to look at the situation too clearly. We have to be willing to face the reality of what went wrong. We have to get really specific about it, and we have to acknowledge exactly what it cost us. That way, we'll be motivated to learn from the mistake we made, and we'll also be powerfully motivated to avoid making the error again.

Immediate Action: When you're launching a new plan and you run into problems, remember the four words to say are, "I can take it." And the next three words to say are, "No matter what!" When I face a major challenge, I say to myself, "I'm going to find out how to solve this. I'm going to win this one." I've learned that no-limits people are committed to learning from problems; they're not intimidated into letting problems turn off their information-gathering systems. They rub their hands together and say, "I can hardly wait to get at this problem." They make the process exhilarating and use excitement to get past the shaking-knees syndrome.

Points to Ponder Before You Go On: "Adversity, if for no other reason, is of benefit, since it is sure to bring a season of sober reflection. Men see clearer at such times; storms purify the air."
—Henry Ward Beecher, American preacher, orator, and lecturer

"A crisis must never be experienced—for the second time."
—Peter Drucker, leadership expert

Chapter 51

Rainbow Moments

"Clouds pass away but the blue heaven lingers on."
—J. Allen Boone, in *Letters to Strongheart*

E ach of us is bound for a unique destination in this life. Flying there is a lot more fun than walking there. Even the moments of fear along the way can be put into perspective if you're willing to ask yourself, "What are my 'rainbow moments'?" I call my own to mind regularly, especially when I'm called on to address tough problems.

When I encounter a problem, I remember the times I've been completely encircled by a rainbow. Not just half a rainbow, mind you, but the full circle. Most of the people I mention this feeling to assume that I'm talking about a half-rainbow, the kind that looks like a "C" tipped forward, with two "legs" touching the ground. I'm talking about the kind of rainbow that goes full circle and looks like an "O." But the only way to see that kind of rainbow—called the "Pilot's Halo"—is to fly low above a flat cloud cover, an undercast.

The clouds have to be flat so they make a deck for you to fly above. You roll up in a turn so that the sun is coming through the canopy of your plane and falling on the cloud deck below. That casts a perfect circular rainbow with the silhouette of your airplane exactly in the center. Wow! What a sight! It was kind of like the Great Squadron Commander in the Sky saying, "I'm here, and here's a little something for you to remember."

The barrier-breaker needs moments like that. You need rainbow moments that remind you of the guiding force behind every adventure that's taking place in life. Your rainbow moments should be ones that remind you of why you do what you do or what you should be doing—and encourage you to recommit yourself to your own highest aspirations. You'll know your own rainbow moment when you encounter it. It's the experience that makes you feel as though everything is falling into place as it should, that the problems you face are within your power to resolve, and that the driving force is with you, making sure that events are unfolding as they ought to. Honor those moments when they come your way, and be ready to call them to mind when the situation warrants.

Immediate Action: What rainbow moments have you experienced? Think about it. If one doesn't come to mind, create one!

Point to Ponder Before You Go On: "I have learned that locked within the moments of each day are the joys and peace we seek....The meaning is in the moment. There is no other way to find them. You feel what you allow yourself to feel each moment of the day."
—Alan Cimberg, professional sales trainer

Chapter 52

Concentration in Times of Crisis

"Character consists of what you do on the third and fourth tries."
—James Michener, author

Did you ever run into a problem that you didn't know was going to be a problem until you were going a couple of hundred miles an hour?

I went through my advanced all-weather fighter interceptor training at Moody Air Force Base in Georgia. That's where I flew my first F86 Sabre—an "L" model. The F86L is near and dear to my heart—it was the first airplane I flew supersonic.

Later, I was assigned to Clark Air Force Base in the Philippines. I went over there to fly F86D's. Now, the F86D was an older model. In fact, the D's I was flying should have been retired from the Air Force inventory about five years before I ever "laid a hand on one of 'em."

It had been about two months since I had flown the F86L. I didn't have that much high-performance fighter experience at that time, and none in the F86D. I knew the flight would be a different experience.

This airplane has only one cockpit, so my first flight in it was also my first solo flight in it! Adding to the challenge was the fact that the interior of the cockpit took a little getting used to for me. There were a whole lot of things in different spots from what I was accustomed to in the L.

All the same, I went out for my first flight, lined up on the runway, pushed the throttle forward, and moved the throttle outboard (which lights the afterburner). I felt that tremendous kick in the pants the afterburner gives you, always a real adrenaline boost. About as soon as I felt that kick, I was screaming down the runway. "Feels great," I thought to myself. When I hit takeoff speed, I pulled back on the control stick. It came back only a couple of inches—and stopped. Something was wrong, and getting worse.

The stick was not a straight stick. It had sort of an "S" curve. It came up, curved toward me, and then up again. I looked down and saw that the stick was jammed up against the survival kit, which makes up the (so-called) cushion in the ejection seat.

Now, as I mentioned earlier, I am a short guy. I had adjusted the seat all the way to the top of its track during my preflight inspection, as I always did in the "L," which had only a thin cushion, not a thick survival kit. If I hadn't adjusted the seat, I wouldn't have been able to see everything I was supposed to see. Now that survival kit, hooked up to my parachute, had moved up with the seat when I raised it. Thanks to shortsighted military ergonomic design, the control stick was banging against the survival kit, as my speed continued to build past liftoff speed.

When you hit that speed, you definitely want to get the airplane into the air. If you have to hit that net (called the "barrier") that stretches across the departure end of the runway, you want to hit it perfectly straight on, or you can slide sideways, dig a wing in the dirt, and flip over. It's real difficult to lift a plane that size off of you if it lands on top of you! And here I was, heading for that net, with a couple of tenths of a second to get my airplane pointed up without using my control stick. This was an interesting situation.

I had about a heartbeat and a half's worth of time to come up with a good answer to the question, "How else can I get this airplane airborne before I engage the 'barrier'?" Fortunately, I didn't waste any time being terrified, or cursing out the guy who'd designed the plane, or wondering what I'd say when I landed. Fortunately, things got real clear, real quick. There was no other choice! I used the "thumb" trim tab on the top of the control stick to reposition the elevator (the horizontal tail surface) to get a little more lift, and "trimmed" the airplane off the ground. I missed the barrier by inches. I gradually gained enough altitude so that I could lower the seat and enjoy full movement of the control stick.

The only problem now was that I was sitting pretty low—make that very low—in the cockpit. I needed a "booster chair" for my booster chair, if you know what I mean! "In a few minutes," I thought to myself, "I'm going to have to land this thing. I sure hope

I'll be able to see everything I need to as I come in." I came in (I didn't know my neck could stretch that far up) and touched down on the end of the runway without incident. My buddy, who was in the little glass shack out at the end of the runway, said about all he could see over the canopy rail was the top half of my crash helmet, about from my eyelids up.

After taxiing in and "deplaning" (as flight attendants now say), I walked in to my flight commander and said, "Anything you want to tell me about that ejection seat?"

"Oh, yeah," he said, "don't raise it all the way to the top or it will interfere with the control stick."

"Yeah," I said. "I'll try to remember that." There was a pause. Then he noticed that I had the deep marks from my oxygen mask on my face.

"You just had a flight, didn't you?" he asked sheepishly.

"Yep," I said.

"Did you have a problem?"

"I had a problem," I admitted, "but it's all right. From now on, though, I'm taking two seat cushions into that cockpit."

And believe me, I did. I was known throughout the Far East as "two-cushion" Cox.

This is just one of the times when I learned that you have to be prepared to respond creatively—and intuitively and immediately—even in totally unexpected situations. You have to be able to respond even when what you have always been able to count on can't be counted on. In moments like that, it's tempting to start focusing on what doesn't work and on how you feel about the fact that it doesn't work. But you can't. You have to be willing to track down what does work first, and with a little help from an adrenaline rush, give the solution all of your attention. That's the only way to solve a critical problem: to focus on it with everything you've got and ask, "How can I make this work?"

Then, after you land your plane, you can go check in with your flight commander!

Immediate Action: Emergencies can sometimes have a marvelous way of summoning the best from people, but it doesn't hurt to plan ahead. Accept that, when you launch a plan to achieve a goal, you will run into problems. Give some real thought to what problems you no doubt will experience, then give some thought to the solutions that will overcome those problems. In other words—prepare!

Point to Ponder Before You Go On: "Adversity has the effect of eliciting talents which under more prosperous conditions may have remained dormant."
—Horace Bushnell, American Congregationalist minister

Chapter 53

Creativity: The Driving Force for Problem Solving

"You cannot depend on your eyes when your imagination is out of focus."
—Mark Twain

Mike Vance and Diane Deacon—founder and president of the Creative Thinking Association, respectively—are two of the world's most creative people. A while back, they spent the day with my wife and me in our library. I passed along some of the antique books from my collection for them to look at. I love to hand people old books and see what passages they find fascinating. As we were digging through the books, sharing things that caught our eye, Mike said suddenly, "You know what we're doing? We're working!" he said with a twinkle in his eye, "And we're having fun!" Mike was absolutely right. For years, he has been a proponent of the principle that "Work should be play, and play should be work." When we took the time to explore those old books together, we were engaged in a mini-vacation—and a very productive one, at that!

The point is, you need a change of pace in your work day. When you notice that your productivity is slowing down, take a lesson from Edison: "Develop the ability to turn from one form of action to another without wasteful friction, and making the second action rest you from the first." Creatively managing the flow of activities from one form to another can provide you with the lift you need to continue your productivity.

Many barrier-breakers have proved that divisions between "work" and "leisure" are really only artificial distinctions. If your leisure time doesn't support who you are when you're at work, it's not going to be much fun for you. If what you do at work is only a way to fill time before 5 p.m. rolls around, then you're going to have trouble achieving at the no-limits level. The same principle applies, in some situations, to the barrier between "ideas" and "execution."

Once, on a trip to Arizona, I visited Taliesen West, the studio of the late, great architect Frank Lloyd Wright, which is located in the desert outside Phoenix. It was a breathtaking experience to wander around the scene of some of Wright's greatest breakthroughs. There's something both humbling and inspiring about examining the work-space of a genius.

The man who showed me around the studio had a fascinating observation on Mr. Wright's creative process. He said it was very difficult for Mr. Wright to tell the difference between thought and action; to him, it was all one process. If the priority was high enough to think about it, he often didn't even realize the transition that led him to start working on it.

Some ideas, in other words, are so powerful, so intoxicating, so liberating, that they all but order you to put them into action immediately. And when you follow that instinct, you usually find you're both working and playing—at the same time.

Henry Ford once said that if a person intends to remain always a manual laborer, then he should forget about his work when the whistle blows. But if he intends to go forward and do anything, then he should consider the whistle a signal to start thinking.

Immediate Action: Figure out what leisure activities make you feel alive, alert, and aware—and also support your work goals.

Point to Ponder Before You Go On: "There are two kinds of dreamers: There is the dreamer who never wakes up; and there is the dreamer who is never so wide awake as when he dreams."
—John W. Cavanaugh, writer

Chapter 54

When Your Salvation Becomes Your Problem

"There aren't any rules around here! We're trying to accomplish something!"
—Sign that hung in Edison's laboratory

Sometimes, what's usually your best weapon starts to work against you. Maybe something you usually count on to deliver superior results—say, a capacity to identify potentially serious errors—is suddenly not what you need. When your company president sits down with you on the first day of the fiscal year to identify and outline his—and your—goals for the year, you may want to give that instinct to instantly identify minor inconsistencies a break. What other skills can you bring to bear to get the most out of the situation? There's a time to track down mistakes and there's a time to take notes. To be a barrier-breaker, you need to know when to back away from one strength and let another take over. This is a matter of practice, of course, but if you develop a talent for knowing when what used to work well, won't work, you'll keep yourself out of trouble. There's nothing more demoralizing than watching the dog that used to hunt for you take a bite out of your ankle.

Twice while landing—once on ice and once while hydroplaning in a heavy downpour—I landed my big, sleek, 70-foot-long, 22 1/2-ton fighter at a hair over 200 miles per hour and found that my drag chute, which normally slowed me down quickly, had decided to act like a huge sail. In both cases, the crosswind turned me sideways, and my plane was sliding down the runway sideways—again, at around 200 miles an hour. This is *not* good.

So what was ordinarily my salvation, the drag chute, was now my problem. I got rid of the immediate problem easily enough by releasing the chute. But now I had a new problem: How would I straighten the plane out? Fortunately, I had a moment of clarity that allowed me to come up with a strategy for dealing with the problem of what to do when my best friend, my drag chute, got into a bad mood. By very, very carefully tapping the rudder pedal, I knew I could use my skidding air speed to swing the plane around and come to a stop.

A good friend of mine once found himself in a worse situation on a very icy, snowy runway: He found himself sliding *backwards* down the runway, completely reversed! He, too, had a moment of clarity, one that helped him develop an effective "instant plan." My friend got rid of the drag chute, just as I had—but my plan wouldn't have done him much good. He wasn't interested in finessing the plane back into position—he had to keep himself on the runway, otherwise he could have ended up in a ball of fire!

This intrepid pilot carefully throttled up the aircraft's power, so that the "forward" thrust of the airplane stopped it from sliding backward. There's an instance of something that's usually your enemy during landing—the jet's forward thrust—becoming an ally. It worked. Quick thinking saved that plane from winding up plowing dirt—or worse. All the same, my friend received some pretty intense attention from the crash crew when he came to a stop. The crew checked that the pilot was all right, which he was. There was a lot of excited chatter. People were pretty impressed with this guy's on-the-spot problem-solving skills. They should have been.

Problem solving under intense pressure can save your hide in a tough situation, but it isn't always fun for everyone involved. Take that backwards-down-the-runway incident. After a few minutes of back-slapping and celebration, someone noticed that the other member of the crew—the radar observer—was missing. The rescue personnel looked inside the plane and all around, but there was no sign of him. Then an eagle-eyed member of the crash crew noticed a trail of footprints leading away from the snowy edge of the runway. The crash crew dutifully followed the footprints and found the radar observer in the officers club. After the miracle landing, he had slipped quietly out of the plane and headed for the nearest bar! He was in the process of encouraging the bartender to "overserve" him.

Immediate Action: Remember that problems aren't always what they seem—and that they're part of everyday life, not something we can isolate ourselves from. Keep in mind that, often, even solutions can eventually become problems.

Point to Ponder Before You Go On: Things that are ordinarily your salvation really can become your problem in an instant. Barrier-breakers don't automatically apply what "usually works" to situations that demand new approaches. They take a deep breath, look past fears and anxieties, launch a "moment of clarity," discover the new reality, and find a new solution to the problem. It takes a person who is confident in his ability to think creatively and function quickly in such a situation to come up with the right solution at the right time. Don't forget, though: The no-limits person wasn't born that way. He or she came up with a response that arose out of instincts that had been developed through many failures and successes.

Chapter 55

Thinking About It Can Be Harder Than Doing It

"Ironically, when people know they must concentrate on a task, they often fail because they make the mistake of concentrating on concentration. They focus on the mechanism of getting the job done rather than the objective itself, which only leads to further distractions....Avoid thinking about the consequences of not getting the job done or how the result will be viewed by others. An Olympic bobsled racer, for instance, was plagued by trouble on a tough curve because he had once crashed there, and he reacted to thoughts about the possibility of a crash, what happened on past runs, and the performance of competitors. When he concentrated only on what he had to do—millisecond by millisecond—to take the curve perfectly, his problems disappeared."
—Dr. Ari Kiev

When I was a manager, I had a salesman named Frank who worked for me. Now, Frank had had a great first year. He'd made plenty of sales, but each time he would close a sale there would be some new kind of headache to deal with. (If you're in the sales field, you already know that this can and does happen.) The problems kept mounting, and by his second year with us, he came to associate the act of making sales with various logistical problems.

At some level, Frank somehow developed the idea that if he made a sale, he would have another set of hassles to contend with. My own feeling was that he amplified and exaggerated the potential difficulties that might arise after he'd sold a property. He spent so much time worrying about the problems he'd encounter after he closed a sale that he actually started holding back during the sales process, and then going home and telling his family about how hard he had worked and how bad his luck had been. We had to work long and hard to get him focused on the positives of what he was doing, rather than on an exaggerated version of the negatives.

Don't confuse pointless worry once you've launched your plan for "strategizing." Don't let thinking about a tough task take away the strength you need to complete that task. As some pundit once said, "Do your worrying before the race—not after you have placed your bet and the horses are coming down the home stretch."

Immediate Action: Think about a time when worrying about an outcome took more time and energy than actually undertaking the task itself. How much easier would it have been for you to tackle the job straightforwardly, without fretting and fuming?

Point to Ponder Before You Go On: *"You Can—But Will You?"*
—Title of a book by Orison Swett Marden

Chapter 56

Quiet Time

"Angels whisper to a man when he goes for a walk."
—Anonymous

The English author Edward Gibbon said, "Conversation enriches the understanding, but solitude is the school of genius." We lose sight of the importance of taking time to ourselves every now and then. Time alone is the foundation of personal creativity—and creativity is essential to good problem solving.

Barrier-breakers know that they need time alone to reflect, observe, plan, and simply be themselves for a while. I've dealt with enough successful people to believe that anyone who expects to become a high achiever should be able to build 15 to 20 minutes of absolute quiet into his or her day, every day and preferably early in the morning. Don't argue—just try it. Chances are, you'll come to enjoy it. It's like looking at the map before the trip, as opposed to looking at it after a day of driving. A 15-minute patch of silence is a minimum "dose" for those of us who face problems on a daily basis. We need to be able to disengage from the pressures of the moment, from the demands that other people place on us, from the sounds of activity and haste that surround the business world. We need to be able to focus on our challenges in absolute silence for a time. If we do, we'll often find that the new approaches we need to make in order to make sense of the problems that face us will reveal themselves to us more or less on their own. But if we don't build silence into our day, we may find that we have lost the ability to listen to the voice that is giving us the answers.

This quiet time should be used to reflect on what we're doing, who we are, and where we're going—without hearing our own voices or anyone else's (or the telephone or the television or any other stimulus). That silence is essential to reflection, and it's definitely essential to developing good problem-solving skills.

But once-a-day quiet time is not enough. We need what I call "mountaintop interludes"—moments when we can really spend some time thinking through our own dreams and developing new ideas about where we're going and how we're going to get there. You might choose to take your day of solitude during a hike up a mountaintop. That's a wonderful way to go. So is a day by the seashore. So is a day in the woods.

I encourage everyone to spend at least two days a year to just be alone and think—to be all by themselves. For me, that's one day in the spring and one in the fall. Each is a day of complete silence to restore and rebuild the self and to address the pressing problems I've been unable to resolve in recent months. No broadcasts of football games. No telephone calls. No deadlines. Just a day to evaluate where I've been, where I'm going, and what the best ways are to get there.

So pick your day. Go someplace where you can relax and just sit and think, uninterrupted, for a full day. Take a pad of note paper or a drawing pad. Take an inspirational book. Whatever you choose to distance yourself from the everyday concerns you face, use that, and devote the entire day to being with yourself, attentively and completely. Just sit there and think and take notes on anything—yes, anything—that pops into your mind.

And by the way, solitude is very different from isolation. A lot of people think that because I say you need mountaintop interludes—or seashore interludes or forest interludes—that I mean people need to be isolated from the rest of the world. That's not what I mean at all. Loneliness expresses the pain of being alone; solitude expresses the glory of being alone.

What I'm talking about are twice-a-year experiences, where you really think about your own strengths, and then daily periods of silence. You can find a way to work them into your day. (If you're tempted to say, "No, I can't," then that's a barrier you can start to work on now!)

Isolation is aimless, painful, exhausting, and limiting. Solitude is productive, joyous, energizing, and absolutely essential to no-limits achievement. Make sure you're using solitude to enhance your own creativity and sense of well-being by putting "time for myself" on your own list of things to do. Why? Because creativity is the clear voice heard in silence.

Immediate Action: Start today—try at least 10 minutes of absolute silence. Stop talking, turn off the radio, television, or computer and simply listen to yourself think.

Point to Ponder Before You Go On: Sometimes a problem situation is a "Master Teacher in disguise," an opportunity for you to relax, step back, take counsel with yourself, and learn something new and important from the situation you face.

Chapter 57

Creative Environments

"The cure for grief is motion. The recipe for strength is action."
—Elbert Hubbard

If you're interested in making the most of your problem-solving abilities, start out by creating a space where you can feel creative. The environment you surround yourself with, both at home and at work, has a direct impact on the creativity of the life you live. That doesn't mean that you have to be able to afford a mansion before you can begin to support your own personal growth. All it means is that your surroundings should be arranged intelligently and in such a way as to stimulate you and support your aspirations.

Through the years, I've noticed that barrier-breakers have demonstrated a special care for the living spaces they've selected for themselves. They use their homes and work environments as more than places to live, but as places that are inspirational to them. My wife and I have a goal to follow their example.

Barrier-breakers know that their surroundings have a huge impact on what they accomplish in their lives. Mike Vance, whom I've mentioned earlier in this book, has to be one of the premier creative thinkers of our time. He was an important contributor to many ideas within the Disney organization. He and his associate, Diane Deacon, paid us the ultimate compliment during a visit when he told us, "You have turned your entire home and garden into a Kitchen for the Mind! That's Mike's term for a stimulating, creative working environment. To find out more about Mike's ideas on the Kitchen for the Mind, see his books *Think Out Of The Box* and *Break Out Of The Box* (Career Press).

The Kitchen for the Mind remark was high praise coming from someone like Mike. The truth is, though, that we were following

Mike's example when we took on the job of setting up our home and office. We wanted to set up an environment that stimulates us the moment we encountered it. Everything was designed to enhance conscious, purposeful, enriched living.

For instance, we've put a lot of work into our flower garden. It's visible from all but two rooms in the house, and it's the place we feel best about going to when it's time to take some silence, either together or apart. When a challenge comes up and we need some perspective, we know the little walkway through our garden out to the gazebo or arbor is there for us at any time. (Remember the connection between creative problem solving and periods of silence? I use the garden all the time to take some quiet time to myself.)

Another great—and inexpensive—way to build a creative environment is to put all the light switches (other than those hooked up to fluorescent lights) on rheostats that allow you to control the level of the lighting in each room. At night, you can set a great mood by turning the dials so that your family room, for instance, looks like it's glowing, rather than being lit from the outside. That has a major impact on the way you perceive your environment and on what you accomplish in it.

What about your work area? What does it say to you? My office, which features easy access to thousands of books that have made a big difference in my life over the years, is another enriching environment. Magazines, paintings, framed epigrams—they're all there. One of our family goals was to be able to get anything in our hands that we needed, either in our office or any part of the house, within two minutes. We're very close to that goal, which was inspired by a study I read that said the average person spends 150 hours per year looking for things! The ability to track information down easily makes it possible for us to take action on important goals, without being encumbered for too long with the task of locating the materials we need.

I find that the moment I walk into the room, I'm walking with a purpose. I like to think of this room as being similar to the "thinking room" I had set up when I was a district manager. I called it the Imaginar Room. Everyone's been to a seminar room, but not too many people have taken advantage of an Imaginar® Room. This was a place with couches and comfortable chairs and places to put my feet up and think and talk with my managers as a group or individually. Because it was a place where we had done great work before, it was natural that when we went there, we expected that we would do great work again. As a result, the place was magic. If a manager came to me and wanted to talk about a problem, he or she would say, "Let's go down to the Imaginar® Room." The trick is to start associating a certain place with your most creative state of mind and to constantly reinforce that association.

How else can you personalize living and working spaces? Use your imagination! We love to travel. In our living room we created a Cultural Center. We placed all of our books that had to do with travel in that room. We brought in artifacts from our trips around the world. One of our chief entertainments on weekends is to go there after we have worked in the gardens and read. It's a little like taking a mini-vacation all over again! Here there are pictures of the people who have made a difference and events that have inspired our lives, all things that focus on and remind us of what our goals are and what we can accomplish. In other words, we took our existing "living room" and made it a distinctive, comfortable space where people would sit and think and talk to each other. And when we were done with the makeover—which didn't involve buying anything new for our home—we discovered that the space had taken on an entirely new role. It had become one of our creative places. Good ideas suddenly started popping up there, and we found ourselves heading to the "living room" for a discussion whenever we were in need of a breakthrough.

Other rooms you spend a lot of time in need attention, too. In our bedroom, we've hung a sign: "No thinking allowed here." (The motto is from Orison Swett Marden who placed a similar sign in his bedroom.) That's a rule we've committed ourselves to following, no matter how strong the temptation is to do otherwise. The bedroom is a place to decompress, not a place to strategize.

We're constantly improving and revising our creative living and working environment. We're always asking ourselves, "How can we make this room 'say something' to us the instant we step in the door?" That's the way to make a living or working space into more than just "a place to live" or "a place to work." These rooms have been transformed from planks and walls and paint into something very different, something a lot more exciting: a Kitchen for the Mind.

Immediate Action: Ask yourself, "How can I change my working and living environment so that it stimulates me in a positive way the moment I walk into it?" Suppose you couldn't spend any money to change your environment. What would you do?

Point to Ponder Before You Go On: Mike Vance and Diane Deacon offer some great ideas on turning your workspace into a creative, stimulating environment. To find out more about their programs, call 800-535-0030.

Chapter 58

The Power of the Productive Vacation

"Yet keep within your heart
A place apart
Where little dreams may go,
May thrive and grow.
Hold fast—hold fast your dreams!"
—Louise Driscoll, poet

I live a pretty high-intensity life style. I average 1,000 miles of air travel a day, 25 hours of time change a month. When I take a few days off, the airlines send me get well cards.

Long ago, I realized that, in order to keep my balance, I would have to have breaks. Not just "a vacation," but something special to restore and rebuild. So in the summer, we take two weeks off—but this is more than a "vacation."

We don't just lie around soaking up sun. We go someplace interesting and relaxing. We take a stack of books; we read each day, and we talk about what we have read at dinner each night. We walk each other through the books in these dinner conversations. Often, we read biographies of people whose lives and accomplishments we admire. We learn so many interesting things that we want to share what we've discovered with each other over these special dinners. We always have a pad and pencil with us to take notes. (In fact, that's how this book got started.)

These trips are supremely energizing, and they're also highly productive. They blur the line between work and recreation. Every year, for instance, right after Christmas, we go to Tucson for a few days. We stay in the same room each year at the Arizona Inn, and we try to focus on the best way to structure the activities that face us in the coming year. We have always been very creative in that room— it's a pilgrimage of sorts. You owe yourself a special "creative place" that you can take advantage of, too—someplace you visit at a special time when you need to take a special new approach to things. Our thinking always runs like this: We have always come up with great ideas for the coming year when we've gone to Tucson, so why shouldn't we be creative this time around?

Places really can foster creativity, and you don't have to travel to a new and exciting city to learn that for yourself. Do what we did—reconfigure your home. But if you can, schedule a pilgrimage for yourself, a time to visit your special place and to come up with important new ideas for the year to come.

Immediate Action: Schedule your "pilgrimage" now—and pay for it ahead of time, so you have to go when the time comes.

Point to Ponder Before You Go On: You should plan your next vacation to include purpose, adventure, and growth.

Chapter 59

Guiding Voices: Your Spirit of Adventure

Here are a few insights on adventure from some of the world's great Master Teachers.

"There is a legend that when God was equipping man for his long life journey of exploration, the attendant good angel was about to add the gift of contentment and complete satisfaction. The Creator stayed his hand and said, 'No, if you bestow that upon him you will rob him forever of all joy of self-discovery.' "
—Orison Swett Marden

"I would rather be ashes than dust!"
—Jack London, American author

"Anything that leads a man aside from the straight path to his goal is a goat feather...[an] unnecessary distraction...."
—Ellis Parker Butler, American humorist

"Learn to identify 'goat feathers' quickly!"
—Danny Cox

"Now, if you are going to win any battles, you have to do one thing. You have to make the mind run the body. Never let the body tell the mind what to do."
—General George S. Patton

"Men who have blazed new paths for civilization have always been precedent-breakers. It is ever the man who believes in his own

ideas; who can think and act without a crowd to back him; who is not afraid to stand alone; who is bold, original, resourceful; who has the courage to go where others have never been, to do what others have never done, that accomplishes things, that leaves his mark on his times. Don't wait for extraordinary opportunities. Seize common ones and make them great."
—Orison Swett Marden

"We all have a land of Beyond to seek in life. Our part is to find the trail that leads to it. A long trail, and a hard trail maybe, but the call comes to us and we have to go. Rooted deep in the nature of every one of us is the spirit of adventure, vibrating under all our actions, making life deeper, higher, and nobler. There's a whisper of the night wind; there's a star agleam to guide us, and the Wild is calling, calling. Let us go!"
—Fridtjof Nansen, Norwegian arctic explorer

"What another would have done as well as you, do not do it; what another would have said as well as you, do not say it; what another would have written as well, do not write it. Be faithful to that which exists nowhere but in yourself and thus make yourself indispensable."
—André Gide, French author

"To think that we were born red, and died bald, and always took things so seriously."
—Elbert Hubbard

"Three statisticians went hunting. Concealed in the underbrush, they spotted a goose flying overhead. The first fired and went 3 feet above the goose; the second fired and went 3 feet below the goose; the third didn't fire at all, but instead shouted, 'We got him!' "
—Anonymous

"The way of the pioneer is always rough."
—Harvey Firestone

"There are three phases: impossible, difficult, done."
—Frank Crane, American author

There Are No Limits

"The one thing that will guarantee the successful conclusion of a doubtful undertaking is faith in the beginning that you can do it."
—William James, American philosopher and psychologist

"It's the struggle toward a goal that makes [one] happy. It is the game we call life that makes it worth living. It is the capacity for joy and sorrow, work, thirst, rest, toil, love, wildlife, and art. This glorious world is mine. I want to live, to give it all of my best powers which I feel are still lying unused, waiting for an opportunity. I see further ahead a new world to be built, and I want to build it."
—Fridtjof Nansen

"No horse ever gets anywhere until he is harnessed. No steam or gas ever drives anything until it is confined. No Niagara is ever turned into light and power until it is tunneled. No life ever grows great until it is focused, dedicated, disciplined."
—Harry Emerson Fosdick, American clergyman

"We are not responsible for every thought that goes wandering through our mind. We are, however, responsible for the ones we hold there. We're especially responsible for the thoughts we put there. It's time to plant a Dream crop of positive visions. It's time to focus on the positive; to hold an image of what we want; to see, view, play (s'il vous plait) our Dream. Or, worded for our more negatively thinking friends: Don't focus on what you don't want."
—John-Roger and Peter McWilliams, American authors of *Do It! Let's Get Off Our Buts!*

"No problem can stand the assault of sustained thinking."
—Voltaire, French writer and philosopher

"Only those who see the invisible can do the impossible."
—Mrs. C.E. Cowman, American devotional writer

"The only way a man can remain consistent amid changing circumstances is to change while preserving the same dominancy of purpose."
—Winston Churchill

"Men grow when inspired by a high purpose, when contemplating vast horizons. The sacrifice of oneself is not very difficult for one burning with the passion for a great adventure."
—Alexis Carrel, French surgeon

"The only life worth living is the adventurous life. Of such a life, the dominant characteristic is that it is unafraid. It is unafraid of what other people think. Like Columbus, it dares not only to assert a belief but to live it in the face of contrary opinion. It does not adapt either its pace or its objectives to the pace and objectives of its neighbors. It thinks its own thoughts, it reads its own books, it develops its own hobbies, and it is governed by its own conscience. The herd may graze where it pleases, but he who lives the adventurous life will remain unafraid when he finds himself alone."
—Raymond B. Fosdick, American author and administrator

"No tyranny of circumstance can permanently imprison a determined will."
—Orison Swett Marden

"Don't get scared by ghosts that ain't."
—Anonymous

"Man is placed into this world not as a finality, but as a possibility. Man's greatest enemy is himself. Man in his weakness is the creature of circumstances; man in his strength is the creator of circumstances. Whether he be victim or victor depends largely on himself."
—William George Jordan, author

Part 4:
Your Desire For Continued Personal Growth

Chapter 60

If Your Life Isn't Unfolding, It's Folding Up

"The person God folded up in you should be unfolded."
—Orison Swett Marden

Too many lives are like an unfinished house. The foundation is there, the walls are up, but where's the roof? Successful people know that a commitment to a better way of life requires all the elements. A desire for continued personal growth is the necessary third part of the no-limits life style—the roof on the house, if you will. It's what gives you a successful future no matter how long you live.

For me, the most important part of that desire for growth has to do with stretching mental horizons—learning new things, meeting new people, discovering new applications. Intellectual growth is only one part of the picture, of course; spiritual and physical progress are important elements of the no-limits life style, too. All the same, intellectual development is the main focus of this part of the book, because it's the type of growth that virtually everyone can learn to embrace with vigor, regardless of age, physical condition, religious or moral beliefs, or even recent history.

Barrier-breakers know: You're never too old—or too young—to stop learning. And they also know that you're never too old—or too young—to ask the question, "What can I learn, or learn to do, that will help me to become a better, happier person?"

This third driving motivation of no-limits achievers very often leads you right back to the first. It reinitiates the whole cycle. Your desire for continued personal growth reinforces your goal orientation in a constructive, positive way, strengthens and enriches your sense of purpose, and even helps you fine-tune (or, if you wish, revise) your goals over time.

Immediate Action: Take a look at the last 10 books you read from start to finish. Ask yourself, "Is this list representative of where I want to develop growth in myself as a no-limits person?"

Then: Read 20 pages a day of a book that's in line with what you want to accomplish. If you do, you can read more than 30 books a year!

Point to Ponder Before You Go On: "A man's reach should exceed his grasp, or what's a heaven for?"—Robert Browning

The Art of
Borrowing Heroes

"One does not change without a model."
—Bruce Larson, minister and author

Have you ever heard the expression "a day at the beach?" I never imagined that wondering about hypothetical "days at the beach" could help to inspire me to new levels of personal growth—but it did.

Early in our friendship with Jim and Ellie Newton, Theo and I were on the beach together, talking about them. I said "Wow, those are great people. What a great thing it would be to just spend a day on the beach with them, with no interruptions." Well, that particular event has in fact come to pass many times in our friendship, and those days on the beach have been very rich and rewarding days indeed.

But on that early occasion, I said, "Let me ask you something—if you could spend 10 days on the beach with the 10 most inspiring people for you, the 10 biggest heroes in your life, living or dead, who would those 10 people be?" We worked the lists out separately.

What an eye opener that game was! And what a great way to focus in on the personal growth issues that made the biggest difference to each of us! I learned a lot about Theo that I didn't know. She learned a great deal about me, too.

The best way for a couple to use that exercise is for each person to make the list separately and then for each person to try to guess who is on the other person's list. If you can guess three selections from your spouse's or significant other's list, you're doing very well. More than three—you have a very rich relationship; less than three, it's a pretty good bet that there is room for meaningful growth. (By the way, this game can be a great way to work on the three lists of Yours, Mine, and Ours goals discussed later in Chapter 68.)

That night, we came up with another variation of the game that involved some additional questions. Using these questions, we came up with an exciting new way to construct a unique personal development course. In addition to asking yourself (or someone else) about the 10 people you'd spend a day on the beach with, consider asking the following questions.

Limiting the second list to living people only, and not repeating anyone from your previous list, who are the 10 people you would want to spend a day with on the beach? The object is not only to imagine interacting with these people, but to use their thinking and the stories of their lives to map the course of your own life. If these are public figures, you can find newspaper and magazine stories, videos, books, audiotapes, and other documentation to learn about their thoughts and actions. With the rise of the World Wide Web you can develop an extensive data file on most public figures—past and present—without ever leaving your computer!

Now ask yourself, "What is the most interesting thing about each of the people on both of the lists I've developed?" Write down the answers; limit yourself to a single sentence for each person. This is a great tool for focusing your study of the individuals you've selected. For example, Winston Churchill was one of the people on my first list. He was a great leader in many, many ways, of course, but the thing that was most interesting to me about Churchill was that he was a great speaker; he simply mesmerized people. When I began to look for information about Churchill as a speaker, I discovered that John F. Kennedy had also admired him for this very reason. I came across a marvelous Kennedy quote about Churchill as an orator: "He mustered the English language," Kennedy once wrote, "and marched it into war." That's as apt a description of what I admire about Churchill as anything I've ever come across!

Next, ask yourself, "Why would any one of those people enjoy spending the day on the beach with me?" As long as you pick someone whose values inspire you and make you want to learn more, there's a good possibility that both of you *would* enjoy the time together. Find the likely points of common ground.

Although meeting the people on your list isn't necessarily an objective, imagining how such a meeting would be is a valuable way for you to learn from them. This is what Mike Vance refers to as "borrowing heroes"—learning from people you admire but never get to meet face-to-face.

And here's a final question to ask, one you should be familiar with already now that you're at this point in the book. Once you've developed your lists and answered questions about both your selections and your own traits, ask yourself, "If I had four more hours per day—28 instead of 24—what could I do to spend those four extra hours that would help me move closer to the example of one of the people on my list?"

By making a habit of, for instance, getting up before the sun does each day, letting your phone machine take messages and then checking them at set points during the course of the day, taking on new aspects of a task so that you spend less time being bored or spinning your wheels, or using any of the other time management techniques we've discussed in this book, you can win back those four hours every day, or something very close to that amount of time. Those kinds of time techniques are exactly the "tricks" employed by barrier-breakers through the years. But to do any of those things, you have to be willing to take personal responsibility for getting organized.

There are many different strategies to consider when it comes to winning back those precious minutes. For instance, you might spend half your lunch hour reading, instead of chatting with co-workers. You might learn to take a 20-minute shower in 10 minutes. You might get up a little earlier. You might improve your delegation skills as a manager. You might simply walk from one place to another faster—a step that will not only improve your daily schedule, but will also help you enjoy a brisk workout! (I often suggest that we develop a "get there gait" by walking at least 25 percent faster during the course of the day. Try it yourself and see how it feels.) You might decide that some part of your daily routine could be better spent. (I know people who complain about how little time they have, and who still manage to watch four and a half hours of television a day—more than a quarter of their waking hours!)

Keep in mind that this four hours of recaptured time won't come in one block. It will no doubt be scattered through the day. Keep no-limits learning material at hand at all times—an audiotape or a biography, say—so you can spend your lunch hour with a person on your list, rather than with a co-worker who always wants to talk about his or her favorite television show. These little "visits" with your inspirational heroes can serve as refreshing breaks from the normal tasks of your job. You receive one-on-one "coaching sessions" from the great achievers you have selected.

Think about it: You have exactly the same amount of hours in your day as any of the people on either of your lists: da Vinci, Beethoven, Edison, Ford, Schweitzer, or Einstein. The question is, how can you manage your day in such a way as to make every minute count, including quality time with your family? Be as specific as you can with your answers.

Those big questions we came up with gave us the opportunity to develop lists that helped us clarify the areas where we wanted to grow. They helped us identify the people whose behavior comes closest to matching the kinds of lives we wanted to pursue. I recommend this game highly to anyone—married or not—who is interested in these topics.

The lists of admired people should be ongoing works; they're never truly finished. You can (and should!) decide to take people off your list. Often, when you research someone in depth, you find that you've found a superior example of how not to do something. Sometimes, too, you remove people from your list simply because you've learned all you want to learn from that person.

Keep the old lists, but be prepared to update your current list regularly (say, every three months) to remind yourself of where you'd like to grow next—and how a hypothetical "day on the beach" can help you get there! This exercise gives you a goal that will help you keep your learning constant.

Immediate Action: To recap: Either on your own or as an exercise with your spouse or partner, write down the answers to the questions outlined in this chapter. Here they are again in condensed form:

1. If I could spend 10 days on the beach with 10 great people (one person per day), asking whatever questions I wished, what 10 people, living or dead, would I pick?

2. Now, what 10 *different* people would I pick—only this time, the group must be composed entirely of living people?

3. In one sentence, what facet of each one of these people's personalities or achievements do I find most attractive?

4. Why would any one of these 20 people enjoy spending the day on the beach with me?

5. From here on, I have 28 hours a day, not 24. How would I spend those four extra hours?

Point to Ponder Before You Go On: The 20 people you identify through the "Five Questions" exercise become your Master Teachers. Learn as much as you can about them. As William George Jordan said, "We envy the success of others, when we should emulate the process by which that success comes." When a Master Teacher emerges for you as a specialist in a certain area, call that person back (either literally or mentally) for consideration.

Chapter 62

Contributaries— Help Along the Way

"Friends make one outdo oneself."
—Orison Swett Marden

Years ago, the writer Helene Hanff wrote a great book called *Eighty-four Charing Cross Road*. It was about Hanff's long-running correspondence during World War II with a man who ran an antiquarian book shop and lived above it at—you guessed it—84 Charing Cross Road in London. Without ever meeting or speaking on the telephone, Hanff and the shopkeeper became very close friends. The story is quite moving, and it was eventually made into a memorable film starring Anne Bancroft and Anthony Hopkins.

On one trip to London, Theo and I went to visit 84 Charing Cross Road. The sign on the building still said "Marks and Company," but the property was vacant. All the same, it was still a thrill to "burn in" the real-life version of a long-imagined location.

Years later, we were sitting in the living room on a Sunday afternoon reading another Helene Hanff book, and we got to wondering whether she was still alive and well—and whether we could perhaps speak with her. We called information and, lo and behold, there she was with a residence listing in Manhattan. I dialed the number. A female voice answered, and I said, "Hello, are you Helene Hanff?"

She said "Yes."

I said, "I understand you like to hear from your fans." (She'd made this clear in several interviews.)

"Oh, I love to hear from my fans," she answered.

So I told her what an inspiration her writing, particularly *Eighty-four Charing Cross Road*, had been in starting me on one of my "break" activities, collecting old books.

She was absolutely thrilled that she had been an inspiration to me. I told her that my main profession is speaking and that, since I started collecting rare books, I often used observations that I had discovered in my new acquisitions in my talks—something I certainly couldn't have done had it not been for *her* book. She was just thrilled with that.

I said, "May I ask you a favor?"

"Certainly," she replied.

"If I send you a hardcover copy of *Eighty-four Charing Cross Road* and include a self-addressed stamped envelope, would you autograph a copy of the book for me?"

She said she would, so we sent it off and we had the signed copy back within a week with a nice inscription on it.

I tell this story, not to drop names or impress you with my contacts in the literary world (although I'm certainly proud to have made this particular author's acquaintance), but to make it clear that a good many of the public figures you admire are more than happy to hear from the people whose lives they've affected for the better. I've had the same kinds of interactions with many, many successful business people. More often than not, I've found that, if you get to the point and are respectful of the other person's time, you can learn some wonderful things. My philosophy has always been: If so-and-so got to be a millionaire by walking funny, I want to talk to that person and learn how to walk funny!

Seriously, though, it is important to touch base with the people who are important in your life. If you are careful to make it easy for them and not take up too much of their time, even some "big fish" will respond to your questions. Including a self-addressed stamped envelope is very important.

Think of someone whom you admire in your community—then call up and ask to buy that person lunch. Make sure the person understands that you only want to learn, that you're not out to sell anything. Think of a *lot* of people. Make a *lot* of calls. The worst that can happen is that the person you talk to will say no. But the truth is, the person does have to eat, and a certain percentage of the time, the person you reach will be more than happy to spend a brief lunchtime with you. If you are excited about a new idea you know this person is behind, call up and ask, "Could we go out to lunch and talk about that idea you had?" In the meantime, as you think about that upcoming lunch, you're bound to have a number of questions. Write them down. Don't be afraid to share a few of your own insights and brainstorms with this person, but let him or her do 80 percent of the talking. By doing so, you may just be laying the foundations for a true friendship, one that both parties benefit from equally.

It's great to be able to sit down for a half an hour or an hour with one of your heroes, to be able to ask, "How did you get from A to B? What did you do when you reached an impasse in such-and-such an area?"

I believe in establishing mentor relationships throughout one's life. The aim is not to develop a relationship based on adulation or blind submission, but to establish a connection that benefits both sides in the mentor relationship. Each should have a stake in the relationship. There should be a two-way street when it comes to building an ongoing relationship with a mentor.

A couple of words of warning: It is difficult to build a mentor relationship with a high-visibility "superstar." That means that you may not be able to connect with all the people you list in response to your "living heroes" question in the exercise that appears in the previous chapter. Rest assured, though, that there are plenty of worthy mentor candidates who don't show up on the cover of *People* magazine.

Often, when you get together with the people you choose to be your mentors, the synergy develops easily and the sharing of ideas and inspiration is a mutually pleasant experience. When a mentor gets to know you—and trust you—don't be surprised if that person suggests that you get together with someone he or she knows. One mentor often leads to another mentor.

One thing that surprises a lot of people who are hesitant about approaching mentors is that the mentors themselves once had mentors. By reaching out to you, or responding when you reach out, the mentor is continuing a chain of relationships that often stretches back a fair distance. You can end up benefiting, indirectly, from some very important people! Here's an example of my own "mentor chart," or "contributary" chart, as I like to call it:

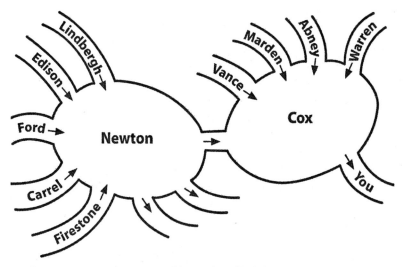

I never met Thomas Edison—he died in 1931. All the same, whenever someone new calls me up and wants to ask my opinion about something exciting, I bring along some of the experience that Edison transmitted to Jim Newton and Jim Newton transmitted to me. I now have the honor of transmitting that information on to someone else!

That doesn't mean I focus only on the new person I've encountered. A lot of people mistakenly think of a mentor as somebody who is going to be a personal coach forever, or that once you pass a certain age, you no longer need a mentor. Wrong on both counts! I call anybody a mentor who has helped me, even if that help came over a brief lunch, even if the person simply helped me to latch on to a single good idea. If what comes out of the meeting is something that I can use, something from which I derive benefit, I call that person a mentor just as much as someone I have kept in touch with over the years. So as I share these ideas from the platform and the printed page, I'm extending the chain—just as you'll be able to do as you build your own chains.

A lot of people shy away from being a mentor because they think that it must be a lifelong commitment. I think this is because many people who seek out mentor relationships seem to misunderstand the nature of the relationship. Successful people are often happy to talk to unfamiliar people, but they do shy away from making the kind of commitment that results in calls at 2 o'clock in the morning. They shy away from people who expect them to share all of their ideas, all of their secrets. They shy away from people who abuse their time, or who offer a constant barrage of questions that are likely to include such queries as "What should I be doing with my life?" or "How can I become a success in your business?" or "How should I deal with this crisis in my marriage?" or "How can I motivate myself?" or "How can I be successful without working hard?" When you contact a potential mentor, you need to make it clear that this is not the kind of relationship that you expect.

Make it clear that you are just reaching out to learn from your mentor. Don't make lots of demands. Take a low-key approach—and if the relationship "clicks" in a way that is mutually beneficial and nourishing, you'll both know it.

Immediate Action: Call up one person you admire and ask to take that person out to lunch. Don't say that you're "looking for a mentor."

When you get face to face with your mentor, consider asking questions like the following:

- How did you get started in your business?
- What separates you (or your company) from your competitors?
- How long had you been in business before you realized you had what it took to be successful?
- What kind of formal education have you had?
- Do you think people can be trained to be successful?
- What influences from the past have been continuing motivators in your life?
- Do you have a guiding philosophy in your life?
- What were your original goals when you were getting started?
- Was there a turning point—a time in your life when you could have "gone either way"? Why did you pick the route you took?
- Have you ever had what you considered a significant failure in business? What did you learn from that experience?

- How many hours do you work per week?
- How do you use your leisure time?
- When and how do you plan your day?
- Do you follow a system in making decisions, and if so, what is it?
- What do you look for in a person who wants to join your company?
- What do you feel is the major hindrance an individual has in achieving his or her potential?
- How have you helped those working for you to overcome that stumbling block?
- Which of your accomplishments do you consider most satisfying?
- What would you regret not having accomplished before you die?

Finally—make darn sure *you* pay for lunch!

Point to Ponder Before You Go On: We live in a cynical age, an age in which many people believe that heroes are no longer necessary. Nothing could be further from the truth. What we don't need are idols—objects of worship who might as well be myths. But we do need heroes. These are real, live people we admire for good reason; people who've accomplished a great deal; people whose examples we would be well-advised to emulate. Our kids need heroes, yes—but so do our grownups.

Chapter 63

Barrier-breakers in Training

"Learn from others' mistakes. You don't have the time to make them all yourself."
—Anonymous

A few years ago I was voted into a group of 20 speakers called the Speakers Roundtable. We get together once a year and share ideas; during the year we send out reports of what's going on in our lives and what trends we are noticing with clients. The main advantage is that we're able to share ideas about how we can get better at what we are doing.

That's a great idea, to find people of like interests, people with the same spirit of adventure, zest for personal growth, and sense of purpose—and get together whenever you can for coffee or lunch. Use that as a support group to explore what's happening in your life as it relates to your most important goals. Take the opportunity to share what you're doing: "Here's what I tried this week, here are the problems I had, and here's what I accomplished because of this."

A word of warning: If that group ever reaches a plateau and ceases to grow (or never starts), you have to be ready to leave it. You can't let anyone pull you back down. So often the self-help groups, particularly those set up for unemployed professionals, become just a pooling of what has not worked. People get up and share their hard-luck stories, one by one. When you get to the end of the hour you have just had a long bath in pure negative thinking. As my friend Stew Leonard says, "Don't walk away from negative people—*run!*"

Immediate Action: Identify (or start) an informal group of barrier-breakers-in-training that makes sense for you—then make the most of it!

Danny Cox

Point to Ponder Before You Go On: "Keep yourself in an ambition-arousing environment."
—Orison Swett Marden

Chapter 64

"Burning in" an Experience

"If there is no strengthening of one's self by a constant intake, there is no help of others by a constant outgo."
—Dr. Frank Crane, author

When you know that you are learning at a peak level, or having special moments of experience, try to concentrate in a special way on those experiences and make sure they register as deeply as possible. That way, the next time you need those lessons, you can take advantage of them with little or no effort. Take full advantage of experiences that contribute to your own personal growth by "burning them in."

I first heard the term "burning in" when Theo and I were with Jim and Ellie Newton. They were walking us through the living room of the historic Thomas Edison house in Fort Myers, Florida. Jim was pointing out all the places where, as a struggling 20-year-old businessman, he had sat and talked with Edison—and Edison, in turn, had shared the riches of his experience with his young friend. Our friend Mike Vance was a few yards behind us, and when we looked at him, we noticed that he was concentrating with all his might.

I wondered whether something might be wrong. Mike looked deeply concerned about something, and so I asked him if everything was all right. He nodded briskly. "I'm burning this in," he said, looking around the room where the great man had done so much living and thinking and barrier-busting. And now, when we go to new places that inspire us or we find ourselves in the middle of an important new learning event, we take special care to burn in the images of our experiences.

You can burn in any experience—positive or negative. It all depends on what you pay attention to with all your might, what you focus on while using all five senses to the limit. You can burn in a feeling of supreme confidence, or you can burn in a conviction that you'll never amount to much of anything. If you have burned in that negative conviction, just remember, you can burn in new and more effective lessons, just as many superior achievers have!

I make a point of burning in life lessons, as well as experiences that are beautiful, awe-inspiring, and capable of making me grateful for the opportunity to grow and learn. For example, not long ago, my wife and I were at our favorite inn, a lovely seaside retreat in Oregon that's situated almost at the Washington state line. (In other words, it's pretty far north.) The last glimmers of the summer twilight extended long after sundown, stretching out to 10 o'clock at night during our visit. We were scanning the panorama, looking at the surf rolling in and crashing against the massive Haystack Rock. The moonlight was lighting up the white tips of the waves. What a sight! We looked at each other and, almost in unison, said, "I'm burning this in!"

Later, we were up at the top of Whistler Mountain in British Columbia, looking down through the valleys there. There was still snow on the ground in July and you could see the clouds sliding down through the valleys below as though they were being ushered along by an invisible hand. We looked at each other, nodded, and said, "Burn it in."

It's not just mountains or seashores that can be burned in. Vivid learning experiences often occur in the humblest of surroundings— and are just as essential. The act of learning itself should be the attraction here, and it should be fun! One of the real treasures of committing yourself to personal growth is that you're committing yourself to something that's enjoyable. Barrier-breakers know that it's enjoyable to expand their horizons; it's even a little bit addictive.

The next time you're learning and experiencing something positive—perhaps even now—burn it in! Make sure it registers in your consciousness and can be used again later.

Immediate Action: Stop and think of the times you've been happiest in your life, when you've felt most fulfilled, most "in the groove." If you're like the tens of thousands of people I've spoken to and trained over the years, you'll think of moments that stretched you a little bit, made you grow, made you look at things in a new way and apply yourself to a problem a little bit differently than you had in the past. Didn't you find that it really was enjoyable to have new and exciting experiences, experiences that make you feel like you're living life the way it ought to be lived? As human beings, we don't like being made to feel as though we were put on the good earth to burrow into a hole and avoid growth. Most people love that exhilarating feeling of expanding horizons. Some train themselves not to enjoy that feeling.

Here's another exercise: Recall any moment in your past—not necessarily a life-changing moment, but simply an event you can remember easily—and "burn it in." Concentrate on the event with all five senses. What did you see, smell, hear, taste, and touch? Once you've made that moment vivid, try to "burn in" a life-changing moment. The bottom line: Don't wait for a peak moment to practice training your subconscious to reexperience key events you select consciously.

Point to Ponder Before You Go On: When we see what's possible, when we meet someone who reminds us, at a very basic level, of what we could be, we usually want to grab that person by the lapels and encourage him or her to sit down with us for a while. If you've ever had the experience of being captivated by a charismatic speaker, you know what I'm talking about. You want to hold onto that feeling that anything is possible. That's only natural. So go ahead! Hold on to new ideas and approaches that work, but take advantage of the times when you stumble on exciting ideas on your own, too. Make a conscious effort to burn it all in.

Chapter 65

Congratulations! You're the Dean of Everyday University

*"The world is a university. Events are teachers. Happiness is
the graduation point. Character is the God-given diploma."*
—Anonymous

Another way of thinking about personal growth is to promote
yourself to the top spot in the most important educational
institution on earth. Actually, no promotion is necessary. The
key is to acknowledge that you already have the job. You are the
Dean of Everyday University (EDU).

You have a chance to learn something every day. It can be
something you see, something you do, someone you talk to. And one
of the very best ways to process this learning, to crystallize it and
make it part of your consciousness, is to talk to somebody else about
what you have learned. As you live your life, if you're using your
learning right, you're in Everyday University. You can learn a life
lesson every day, and if it doesn't happen, it's because you aren't
paying attention—not because the course material isn't there for you
to take advantage of!

Jim Rohn once said, "In order to do more, you have to be more."
He meant, I think, that the standards at EDU have to be high ones.
You have to take advantage of every learning opportunity—both
in your family life and in the business world. Nobody can do that
for you.

To do that, you should make full use of all the new experiences
and new awareness you acquire through EDU and ask yourself a very
simple question: "How can I use what I've just learned to improve
my situation?"

There Are No Limits

The University is a funny institution that way. Its staff and faculty, which report directly to you, aren't interested in simply making you a repository for all the new information that's coming your way. They aren't interested in what someone once called "intellectual taxidermy." They want you to use what you've learned. As the dean, you have to be willing to give the student body (which is also you) a little bit of a lecture from time to time: "Don't tell me what you know, tell me how you're using it." You have to get out there and try things, based on the new information you've uncovered.

That's what's known as the exam period at EDU—trying something new. You must take what you've learned and find a way to improve something with it. Thomas Edison never developed an invention that didn't have a specific practical application. He was always trying to use what he was learning to "pass an exam," to put his ideas to use. Everything that Edison did was supremely practical; he always wanted to see his ideas being used. As dean of EDU, you will want to take exactly the same approach.

Immediate Action: Set up a bar graph describing:

1. Your current earnings.

2. What you could earn with better application of current knowledge.

3. What you could earn with better application and further learning.

Potential Earnings Bar Graph

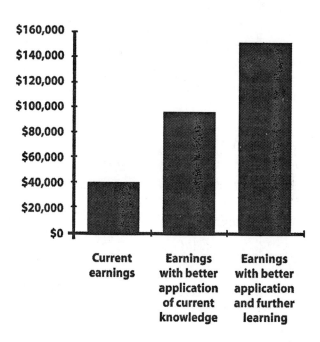

Point to Ponder Before You Go On: "The quality of your life is directly proportional to your commitment to excellence."
—Vince Lombardi

Chapter 66

Leisure Time,
Work Time

"Tell me how a young man uses his little ragged edges of time after his day's work is done, during his long winter evenings—what he is revolving in his mind at every opportunity—and I will tell you what that young man's future will be."
—Orison Swett Marden

What we learn after work determines how well we do at work. What we do at work determines how we feel when we get home. At a certain point, we have to ask ourselves: Is our current life style preventing us from achieving a far, far better way of living?

The life style change we identify may not be easy at first, and it may not be what everyone else is doing. We live in an age when information technology has grown at astounding rates of speed—and when a new "wired" generation can find a World Wide Web site for every obsession, whether it's creative or destructive. We also live in a society where television is king and where an incredible amount of social energy is spent discussing, analyzing, and reliving what happened the night before on a plastic box with speakers, a knob, and a glass display screen. Fortunately, we also live in a country where individual choice still determines how a person spends the day, and where no one has to spend the day hypnotized unless he or she chooses to!

Don't get me wrong—I think the Internet is an amazing research tool. But today, technology has, in too many cases, become a way of quickly dispersing mediocre, mundane thoughts. When the Internet becomes more of a productivity vacuum than a productivity tool, I say it's time to stop wandering around the Internet.

Speaking personally, I want to be "cutting edge" on thought, not "cutting edge" on technology for its own sake. Technology has to be the tool for keeping track of cutting-edge thought. Technology must always come second in line; thought has to be the first priority.

Television, too, has many positive aspects. It's the only place your kids can see Sesame Street and the only way you can see important news events unfold, as they're taking place, from virtually anywhere on earth. Of course, those are important contributions to society. But it will probably come as no surprise to learn that television usually doesn't live up to its full potential as an educational tool or news delivery system. All too often, television is an excuse to "learn" mediocrity—and nothing more. That's why it's not the best centerpiece of any no-limits life style. Barrier-breakers don't let television rule their lives. They use TV sets selectively, rather than letting TV sets use them.

Forty years ago, a character in the theatrical film *The Manchurian Candidate* made this observation: "There are two types of people in the world—those who walk into a room and turn on the television when it's off, and those who walk into a room and turn off the television when it's on." No-limits achievers definitely fall into the latter category! Today, there's a popular bumper sticker that reads, "Kill Your Television." That may be taking matters a step or two too far, but the sentiment is certainly an understandable one. If commercial television is the most important force in determining what's happening during your leisure hours, then your television set should at least be put under heavy sedation!

Immediate Action: The next time you're enjoying a situation comedy on television, make a point of laughing just as hard at the jokes as the laugh track is laughing. You'll convince yourself in short order that sitcoms are not as funny as the "powers that be" would have you believe.

Point to Ponder Before You Go On: "In this interactive world we may be connected to information, and lose our connection to humans."
—Edward Esper, Jr., President and CEO, Creative Labs Inc.

Chapter 67

When Two
Become One

"In real love you want the other person's good. In romantic love you want the other person."
—Margaret Anderson, in *The Fiery Mountains*

[Author's note: The next four chapters are primarily of interest to couples and families. If you're single now, but feel it's likely you will be making commitments in your life at some point, please come back to chapters 67, 68, 69, and 70 later and get more information on family-centered learning.]

One of the best ways you can fine-tune your goals to inspire high performance and long-term growth is to make sure your family—and particularly your partner—is part of the no-limits experience. I believe the commitment you make to your family in pursuing your highest aspirations for personal development must be unwavering if your work is really to amount to anything. My wife and I encountered such a "burnt-in" symbol of commitment the last time we saw Anne Morrow Lindbergh.

We had met Mrs. Lindbergh several times over the years; the occasion I'm thinking of took place in February, 1997. We were invited for dinner at the home of our friends Jim and Ellie Newton in Fort Myers Beach, Florida, and our dinner companion, seated to my right, was Anne, the soon-to-be-91-year-old widow of Charles A. Lindbergh. When Jim, our host, led us in the blessing before the meal, I realized that on the gentle left hand extended for me to hold during the prayer was wearing the wedding band Lindbergh had placed on that hand so many years before. The wedding band I was touching was a symbol of the deep commitment that had guided that couple through so many years—through very good times and very bad times—a commitment to facing life together and growing together, whatever the challenges.

I was reminded particularly, as I held that soft and vulnerable hand, of the trip the Lindberghs had taken together mapping the great circle routes over the frozen north. Those trips are chronicled in Mrs. Lindbergh's book *North to the Orient*. These are the routes still used by pilots today as they fly from cities in North America to China and other far-eastern points!

On the first of these flights, Lindbergh landed the plane in Canada for refueling. When it was discovered that Mrs. Lindbergh was aboard the flight, an astonished attendant blurted out, "I wouldn't dream of taking my wife on such a hazardous adventure." "She's crew!" was his terse—and proud—rejoinder. She was crew; she handled all the radio communications, and sent and received messages in Morse code, throughout the entire perilous journey!

This, I remember thinking to myself, was what a real marriage—a union—looked like.

Immediate Action: Talk, in detail, about something you've learned in this book with the person who means the most to you in life.

Point to Ponder Before You Go On: "Love is a noun. Love is a verb. It was meant to be seen as well as heard."—Anonymous

Chapter 68

"Your Goals, My Goals, Our Goals"

"Too many women see only the weak points in a strong man and the good points in a weak one."
—Elbert Hubbard

"And vice versa!"
—Danny Cox

My wife and I have been blessed with an incredibly happy 30-plus years of marriage, and we've both been inspired to grow and develop constantly. That's at least partly because we have always had three sets of goals: "Her" goals, "His" goals, and "Our" goals.

The growth structure in a marriage is like a three-legged stool. Each of those groups of goals is one leg. If any leg is missing, the stool won't stand up. If the marriage is built around one person's goals, or even around both individual sets of goals, it will be weaker than if there is a third set of goals: the things "we" want to achieve together.

Another part of the integrity of a marriage is understanding the need to be by yourself, the need to have some time alone to recharge your own batteries. There's nothing wrong with that! In fact, I think any happily married couple will tell you that there's something essential about being able to take time to yourself from time to time to dream, to plan, to find out what makes sense for you so you can talk about it in depth later on with your partner. That's not shutting your partner out—that's making sure he or she has a real, live partner who's energized and committed to goals that support a harmonious life together.

In our case, that means I get to focus on my goals, which generally have to do with developing and presenting material to my audiences and readers to help them develop more of their potential. Theo gets to focus on her goals, which often connect with her passion for studying archaeology. Together we focus on mutual goals, which usually have to do with expanding our personal horizons, spending time together, enjoying family time, improving our living space, and similar issues.

Immediate Action: For couples: Develop lists of "your goals," "my goals," and "our goals." Your relationship will be stronger for it!

Point to Ponder Before You Go On: "Love is the ultimate recognition you grant to someone else's superlative values."
—Ayn Rand

Chapter 69

"Forced Family Functions"

"If we suddenly discovered that we had only five minutes left to say all we wanted to say, every telephone booth would be occupied by people trying to call up other people to tell them that they loved them."
—Christopher Morley, author

As our kids grew up and started families of their own, we noticed two important things:

*The girls weren't around as much as they once were, and
We were related to a lot more people than we used to be.*

In order to maintain continuity—and make sure we still enjoyed opportunities for sharing and creativity within the family group—we launched what we call "triple F" nights, which stands for "Forced Family Functions."

That's right, we check our schedules and come up with a day for a "triple F" celebration—for the birthdays that take place in the period of a month or two, for example. The rules are simple: The dates have to be convenient for everyone in the family, and everyone has to be there, no excuses, short of being either a) in the hospital or b) dead.

These mandatory (and joyous!) get-togethers provide us all with a perfect opportunity to bring each other up-to-date on current plans, goals, and challenges. We've made a conscious decision to keep family life a strong and regular part of our lives, even though people in the family are sometimes spread all over the map. The same system may be worth considering in your own far-flung family. For us, there's never a time when the input—and company—of family members won't be essential.

Immediate Action: Schedule a Forced Family Function, where you and your loved ones can assemble and enjoy time together as a family.

Point to Ponder Before You Go On: "We should all have more life-enhancing conversations."
—Margaret Eiluned Morgan, Director, New York Deming Research Group

Chapter 70

Dinner Rituals

"Swallow a lot of fun with your meals."
—Orison Swett Marden

D o you sometimes wish you could communicate more clearly with your loved ones about the most important learning experiences in daily life? If so, try this exercise with your family: Each evening at mealtime, address each of the following questions (penned by an anonymous author many years ago):

What one thing did you see today that was beautiful?
What did you learn today that you didn't know?
How did you help someone today?

Try to get each family member to answer each question. Make the questions part of your evening routine. Knowing that you are going to have to answer the questions each night helps you pay attention to the important things that are happening each day. As you pay more attention to your experiences, your experiences automatically become richer.

When Abraham Maslow talked about developing the "self-actualized" person, he said that the key to self-actualization is awareness. If knowing that you are responsible for answering these questions helps you to become more aware during the course of the day, consider using this three-question exercise.

Immediate Action: Ask—and answer—the three dinnertime questions daily, either with a loved one or by committing your answers to a personal journal.

Point to Ponder Before You Go On: As a wise person once observed, children are a far more likely to follow your lead than to walk in the direction you point.

Chapter 71

Guiding Voices: Your Desire for Continued Personal Growth

Here are insights on personal growth courtesy of some of the world's great Master Teachers.

"[Jim Newton] says he intends to keep growing until he leaves the planet. It is doubtful that the process will stop then. Wherever he is headed, they probably can use a good real estate man. With his skills and his record of shoe horning the right people into the right dwelling, they could keep him busy for quite a while. After all, Jim Newton has read somewhere that in his father's house 'there are many mansions.'"
—Willard Hunter, speaker/author

"Just three days shy of his 89th birthday, [Norman] Vaughan reached the summit of the mountain that bears his name....It was a climb the octogenarian had been planning for 66 years, ever since Adm. Richard Byrd named the 10,302-foot Queen Maud Mountains peak Mount Vaughan. Vaughan, then a 22-year-old Harvard dropout, was chief dog musher for Byrd as he led the first expedition to the South Pole in 1928....[T]he remote Mount Vaughan remained inaccessible to its namesake until the late 1980s, when a private adventure travel company established air service to the mountain's base."
—*Orlando Sentinel*, January 7, 1995

"Things for which you are searching, may well be searching for you."
—F.D. Van Amburgh, author

There Are No Limits

"An unused mind devours itself."
—Gore Vidal

"The world bestows its prizes, both its money and honors, on one thing and that's initiative. What is initiative? I will tell you. It is doing the right thing without being told. But next to doing the thing without being told, is doing it when you have been told once. That's carrying the message to Garcia. Those who can carry a message get high honors but their pay is not always in proportion. Next there are those who never do a thing until they are told twice. Such get no honors and small thanks. Next there are those who do the right thing only when an executive kicks them from behind, and these get indifference instead of honors, and a pittance for their pay. This kind spends most of its time polishing a bench with a hard luck story. Then still lower down the scale than this we have the dullard who will not do the right thing even when someone goes along to show him how and stays to see he does it. He is always out of a job and receives the contempt he deserves unless he happens to have a rich Pa in which case destiny patiently awaits around the corner with an [iron] club. To which class do you belong?"
—Elbert Hubbard, from the prologue to *A Message to Garcia*

"Remember these are men. They feel elation, fear, and joy—especially joy. They do a joyful thing here. And even if we only watch, we have some of that joy and excitement injected into our lives."
—Frank Herbert, *Threshold: The Blue Angels Experience*

"All that mankind has done, thought, gained, or been is lying in matchless preservation in the pages of a book."
—Thomas Carlyle, Scottish historian and philosopher

"If you're not growing, you're not going."
—Sam Walton

"It is told of Leonardo da Vinci that while still a pupil, before his genius burst into brilliance, he received a special inspiration in this way. His old and famous master, because of his growing infirmities of age, felt obliged to give up his own work and one day bade

da Vinci finish a picture which he had begun. The young man had such reverence for his master's skill that he shrank from the task. The old artist, however, would not accept any excuse but persisted in his command saying simply, 'Do your best.' Da Vinci at last tremblingly seized the brush and, kneeling before the easel, prayed, 'It is for the sake of my beloved master that I implore skill and power for this undertaking.' As he proceeded his hand grew steady, his eye awoke with slumbering genius, he forgot himself and was filled with enthusiasm for his work. When the painting was finished, the old master was carried into the studio to pass judgment on the result. His eye rested on a triumph of art. Throwing his arms around the young artist he exclaimed, 'My son, I paint no more.'"
—from *Streams in the Desert* by Mrs. Charles E. Cowman

"I believe in the stuff I am handing out, in the firm I am working for, and in my ability to get results. I believe that honest stuff can be passed on to honest men by honest methods. I believe in working, not weeping; in boosting, not knocking; and in the pleasure of my job. I believe that a man gets what he goes after, and that one deed done today is worth two deeds done tomorrow, and that no man is down and out until he has lost faith in himself. I believe today in the work I am doing, and tomorrow in the work I hope to do, and in the sure reward which the future holds. I believe in courtesy, and kindness, and generosity, and good cheer, in friendship and honest competition. I believe there is something doing somewhere for everyone ready to do it. And I believe I am ready right now."
—Elbert Hubbard

"The only time you want to look back is when you want to learn something."
—Chuck Yeager

"Welcome change as a friend; try to visualize new possibilities and the blessings they are bound to bring to you. If you stay interested in everything around you—in new ways of life, new people, new places and ideas—you'll stay young, no matter what your age. Never stop learning and never stop growing. This is the key to a rich and fascinating life."
—Alexander De Seversky, designer of Air Force bombers (such as the B-47)

There Are No Limits

"The small mind that magnifies little things cannot grasp great things."
—F.D. Van Amburgh

"Never cease to want to grow up."
—Margaret Eiluned Morgan

"Totaling at today's cost...nature invested one million dollars in every gallon of petroleum we harvest. That is not regenerated like trees and corn. It's short-term capital. Bucky [Fuller] compares it to the food deposited inside the egg to nourish the chick, until it breaks out of the shell and makes contact with the great universe. The chick was not designed to consume that deposit and then starve. Nor were we designed to consume our deposit of coal and oil and then starve. We were designed to start using our minds, eventually."
—Hugh Kenner, in *Bucky*, his biography of Buckminster Fuller, father of the geodesic dome

"A human characteristic is that we refuse to give up the quest for perfection. If you say something is impossible, that challenge is often all we need to make us try the impossible. But men stumble in their thoughts when they imagine such thresholds. Each testing of our limits hides its own dangers and you either have respect for such a crossing or you are dead....To gather the universe into your hands at the moment of crossing—that is triumph....That's how it is with thresholds. They dare us to do our best."
—Frank Herbert, in *Threshold: The Blue Angels Experience*

"'My definition of an ideal personality for business,' says a writer and philosopher, 'can best be given by using the letters PERSONALITY.

P—Perseverance
E—Earnestness
R—Reliability
S—Sincerity
O—Optimism
N—Naturalness
A—Ability
L—Loyalty
I—Initiative
T—Tidiness
Y—Yearning

Perhaps 'Yearning' should come first. It is because of this strong desire for self-improvement, and the wish to do the best in service to herself and her employer, that impels a successful [person] in business to acquire the other qualities that I have mentioned."
—Orison Swett Marden

"Why isn't joy a company staple?"
—Margaret Eiluned Morgan

"Stagnation is evident when the past seems large and more important than the future."
—Elbert Hubbard

"I don't think much of a man who is not wiser than he was yesterday."
—Abraham Lincoln

"Solon, the sage of Athens, was asked the secret of strength and youth. He replied: 'I learn something new every day.'"
—Orison Swett Marden

"Halfway knowledge is all right—if you want to go halfway to your goals."
—E.C. Holman, author

"Lift yourself to the level of your highest gift. Let no man complain that he has been ill-treated by the world until he has made the most of the stock that has been implanted in him by his creator."
—Orison Swett Marden

"Those who are successful are those who have known more than the average person considers necessary."
—F.D. Van Amburgh

"It is not enough to have great qualities. We should have the management of them."
—Orison Swett Marden

"When you cease to be better, you cease to be good. When you stop growing, you cease to be useful—a weed in the garden of prosperity.... We are what we are today because we were what we were yesterday. And our thoughts today determine our actions tomorrow."
—George Knox, in Leadership

"A famous, self-made man was described thus: 'He was born mud and died marble.' This gives us an interesting metaphor to use to look at various lives. Some people are born mud and remain mud....Sadly, some are born marble and die mud; some are born mud, dream of marble, but remain mud. But many persons of high character have been born mud and died marble. There are parallels here with the Gospel story of the master who gave various talents to his servants. One squandered the talents and returned with none; one carefully stored the talents and returned them intact at the end; but the servant who received the most praise invested the talents wisely and returned the talents multiplied 10 times."
—Orison Swett Marden

Five...Four...Three...
Two...One...Ignition!

You've reached the end of the book, but your journey to a no-limits life style is really just beginning. I challenge you to devote your attention to something exciting—right now. It could be a new goal, or it could be the first step toward an exciting adventure you've already planned, or it could be a unique learning experience, one that fills you with awe and wonder. Whatever it is, as you use the three forces of no-limits achievers to bring about positive change in your life, you must embrace all three of these forces and commit yourself to positive values if you are to enjoy balance and true success in life.

Some people get stuck on the sense of purpose—they're forever setting goals, but they never seem to accomplish anything. Others become so enamored with adventure that they lose sight of where the adventures are taking them, and they expose themselves to risks that simply don't make sense. And many, many people fall into the trap of viewing the quest for continued personal growth as an excuse for embarking on a lifelong career as a professional student.

True purpose, true adventure, and true growth mean something very different. They require committing yourself to a cause that matters deeply to you, then seeing it through and becoming a better person as a result. That's my challenge to you as we conclude this book: to use all three of the no-limits forces to turn what were once dreams into the reality that is your destiny, the destiny to be the very best person you can be.

Birthplace of a Brighter Future

by Danny Cox

As I concentrate on each word of this thought, "now" slips by me into the past. My past, then, is nothing more than a history of how well I dealt with each irretrievable "now." So if yesterday is history, tomorrow is a prediction. Only the present exists.

The future is nothing more than an approaching series of "nows." During one of these "nows," I must make a decision that all future "nows" will be different. A brighter future grows out of a brighter "now." Therefore, my future improves only as I make better use of the current moment.

It's the time remaining that counts, but just as important is my understanding of that profound truth. My willingness to accept responsibility for improving that time will determine the quality of the rest of my life.

The speed at which "now" becomes the past is staggering. Yet, if I commit my God-given strengths to improving each of these approaching "nows," the faith in my bright new future will be exhilarating! For I realize that the same velocity that carries this "now" into the past can carry me at the same rate toward exciting moments of the future when ever-increasing goals become reality.

A year yet to be is unborn, untarnished, and full of promise. One of those brand-new years—bright with potential, accomplishment, and joy—will be delivered to me tomorrow at dawn. My choice is to accept it as it is given, or through habit, mold it into the shape of years past.

The challenge is clear. The choice is mine. Challenge accepted!

Immediate Action: Fasten your seat belt and plan your new birthday celebration—for one year from now!

A Final Thought: May the rest of your life be the best of your life! Happy new birthday!